An America That Works:

The Life-Cycle Approach to a Competitive Work Force

A Statement by the Research and
Policy Committee of the Committee
for Economic Development

Library of Congress Cataloging-in-Publication Data

An America That Works: The Life-Cycle Approach to a
Competitive Work Force: a Statement by the Research and
Policy Committee of the Committee for Economic
Development.
p. cm.
Includes bibliographical references.
ISBN 0-87186-091-0 (paperback) : $15.00. --
ISBN 0-87188-791-5 (library binding) : $20.00
1. Manpower policy--United States. 2. Human capital--
United States. 3. Age and employment.
I. Committee for Economic Development.
Research and policy committee.
HD5724.A49   1990
331. 12' 042' 0973--dc20

First printing in bound-book form: 1990
Paperback: $15.00
Library binding: $20.00
Printed in the United States of America
Design: Rowe & Ballantine

COMMITTEE FOR ECONOMIC DEVELOPMENT
477 Madison Avenue, New York, N.Y. 10022
(212) 688-2063
1700 K Street, N.W., Washignton, D.C. 20006
(202) 296-5860

TABLE OF CONTENTS

iv

An America That Works:

The Life-Cycle Approach to a Competitive Work Force

RESPONSIBILITY FOR CED STATEMENTS ON NATIONAL POLICY

The Committee for Economic Development is an independent research and educational organization of over two hundred twenty five business executives and educators. CED is nonprofit, nonpartisan and nonpolitical. Its purpose is to propose policies that bring about steady economic growth at high employment and reasonably stable prices, increased productivity and living standards, greater and more equal opportunity for every citizen, and improved quality of life for all.

All CED policy recommendations must have the approval of trustees on the Research and Policy Committee. This committee is directed under the bylaws which emphasize that "all research is to be thoroughly objective in character, and the approach in each instance is to be from the standpoint of the general welfare and not from that of any special political or economic group." The committee is aided by a Research Advisory Board of leading social scientists and by a small permanent professional staff.

The Research and Policy Committee does not attempt to pass judgment on any pending specific legislative proposals; its purpose is to urge careful consideration of the objectives set forth in this statement and of the best means of accomplishing those objectives.

Each statement is preceded by extensive discussions, meetings, and exchange of memoranda. The research is undertaken by a subcommittee, assisted by advisors chosen for their competence in the field under study.

The full Research and Policy Committee participates in the drafting of recommendations. Likewise, the trustees on the drafting subcommittee vote to approve or disapprove a policy statement, and they share with the Research and Policy Committee the privilege of submitting individual comments for publication.

Except for the members of the Research and Policy Committee and the responsible subcommittee, the recommendations presented herein are not necessarily endorsed by other trustees or by the advisors, contributors, staff members, or others associated with CED.

RESEARCH AND POLICY COMMITTEE

Purpose of this Statement

The United States is experiencing population changes that are outpacing the abilities of government, business, and community institutions to cope. Throughout the nation, the gap between job requirements and job skills is growing. Traditional ways of working and managing are also being challenged daily by new global, technological, and social realities.

An America That Works offers a comprehensive framework for examining the relationship between sweeping demographic changes and the world of work. This volume establishes important linkages among the many social and economic issues that relate to demographic change. It also helps set priorities as we adjust to changing circumstances.

The report clearly identifies the changes taking place in the work force and the workplace, the problems of poor basic education and work readiness, the need to expand the pool of available workers, and the challenges these issues pose for U.S. global competiveness. It also offers positive, constructive, and specific actions that the private and public sectors can take so that our nation and our citizens can benefit and prosper from these changes.

Our study devotes considerable research and attention to the effects that changing jobs are having on workers and the effects that changing workers are having on jobs. We conclude that while we can be optimistic about the future, a comprehensive and swift response is critical if needed policy changes are to be made effectively and efficiently.

An America That Works has grown out of CED's long-standing commitment to developing policies to improve the strength and well-being of the U.S. economy. The life-cycle approach to U.S. work force issues we outline here stems from a broad-based body of work CED has produced on productivity and competitiveness.

The foundation for our recommendations on education reform and family policies was laid in our two recent studies on improving public education in this country. In 1985 we issued *Investing in Our Children: Business and the Public Schools* and in 1987, *Children in Need: Investment Strategies for the Educationally Disadvantaged*, both of which have contributed significantly to the education reform movement.

The need for government, business, and workers to respond to rapid changes in the world economy was the theme of CED's 1987 study *Work and Change: Labor Market Adjustment Policies in a Competitive World* which recommended policies to help the U.S. labor market adapt to new employment opportunities.

The CED statements *Investing In America's Future* (1988), *Reforming Health Care: A Market Prescription* (1987), *Leadership for Dynamic State Economies* (1986), and *Reforming Retirement Policies* (1981) have all helped the subcommittee that prepared this report grapple with changing employment practices and other policies that business and government will need to examine.

Also, throughout its deliberations, the CED subcommittee on the work force has tested new ideas and developed conclusions in meetings with key policy makers around the country.

ACKNOWLEDGMENTS

I would like to thank the able group of CED trustees and advisors who served on the CED subcommittee that prepared this report (see page x). Very special thanks go to the subcommittee's co-chairmen, Frank P. Doyle, Senior Vice President of GE, and Rocco C. Siciliano, retired chairman of Ticor, for the wisdom and leadership they brought to this important project. We are also indebted to project co-directors R. Scott Fosler, CED's Vice President and Director of Government Studies, and Jack Meyer, President of New Directions for Policy, for their ability to bring clarity and cohesion to these complex issues.

Thanks are also due to Sean Sullivan, Vice President of New Directions for Policy, and to Carol Alvey and Greg Collins of CED for their important contributions to this project.

We are deeply grateful to The Ford Foundation, the Alfred P. Sloan Foundation, the Kraft General Foods Foundation, The James Irvine Foundation, the General Electric Foundation, The Travelers Companies Foundation, Inc. and the Robert Wood Johnson Foundation for their generous support of this most important program.

Dean Phypers
Chairman
CED Research and Policy Committee

Chapter 1

Introduction and Summary

Many policy decisions, both in business and government, are being made as if the U.S. population, work force, and age and cultural mix will continue to be more or less the same as they are now. Nothing could be further from the truth.

America has entered an era of fewer entrants into the work force and an aging population. This era will be marked by a lower birthrate, a rising average age, increased immigration, and growing ethnic and cultural diversity.

As recently as the early 1980s, there were too few jobs in a slack economy. But, if there is strong future economic growth, some communities may be facing the problem of too few skills for the competitive economy that will demand them. The challenge for business and public policy makers will be to develop qualified workers to fill the increasing numbers of knowledge- and technology-driven jobs. Without an educated, able citizenry, America will suffer lower living standards, with far too many of its people shut out from the opportunities our economy and society will have to offer.

We are already experiencing radical changes in what kind of work is done, how it is performed, and who does it. The rate of change will only accelerate, and it is critical for public and private policy makers to recognize that.

The ability to make the best use of human resources is now a strong competitive edge for both countries and companies. In the new world of fewer workers and higher-value jobs, the advantage will go to those nations and businesses that invest in their people, recognize and remedy underutilized potential, and produce an educated and adaptable population.

Achieving this competitive advantage will require new approaches to education and the management of human resources that emphasize learning, flexibility, and productive participation in work and society throughout the entire life of an individual. Through what we call the *life-cycle approach* (see page 6), we believe policies can be implemented that will help children reach school healthy and ready to learn, prepare young people for rewarding work and community participation, enable adults to be self-sufficient, and help older citizens remain active and independent.

Demographic trends argue for an emphasis on bringing more people into the labor force; yet many of our policies, from welfare to retirement rules, encourage people not to work. Demographic trends call for an emphasis on continuing education and retraining when workers lose jobs, yet, our unemployment policies focus largely on income maintenance. The nature of work is changing and will require greater flexibility and more independent decision making, but many schools and workplaces are still geared to an outdated factory model of rigid segmentation and top-down management.

In the years to come, *employers* will be challenged to attract and retain qualified workers who will enable them to compete effectively in a global economy. *Workers* will face problems of adapting to rapidly changing technology, balancing the needs of a job and family, and adapting to a world in which retirement at 62 or 65 may no longer be the norm. *Government* will be challenged to significantly upgrade the education of America's citizens, to reshape social insurance programs and assure that their costs are kept under control, and to realign incentives to favor productive activity.

In this policy statement, we make specific recommendations for what business and government should do to adapt to and benefit from changing demographic trends. But more important than any business or government activity will be the actions and initiatives of individuals who have a clear responsibility to recognize the value of healthy families, lifelong learning, and long-term planning and to act on these values in their daily lives. Society can and should create opportunities and incentives for individuals to grow, develop, and be productive – in paid or unpaid activities – and to make evident the advantages of doing so. But individuals must seize the opportunities and respond to the incentives.

THE DIMENSIONS OF THE PROBLEM

Now is the time to begin reshaping our public policies, business practices, and social institutions as the baby boomers, the 77 million people born between 1946 and 1964, work their way toward retirement. Behind this group is the "baby bust" generation, a significantly smaller group.

Over the next decade, the rates of growth in the prime working-age population and the retirement population will be roughly equal. This parity is a significant change from the prior 12 years, when the average annual growth of the 25- to 54-year-old group was 50 percent larger than for the 55 and over group (see Figure 1). In the future, we will have relatively fewer working-age people than in the past to support the retired population.

Moreover, this parity in growth between the two age groups is a prelude to a period of much more rapid growth for the 55 and older group than for those 25 to 54 years old. The trend is even sharper for those 75 and over.

Figure 2 shows the effects of different assumptions about population growth on the ratio of those 65 and over to those of working ages 20 to 64. The low-dependency scenario depicted in Figure 2 emerges from a set of

FIGURE 1

Average Annual Population Growth Rates, 1976 to 2000

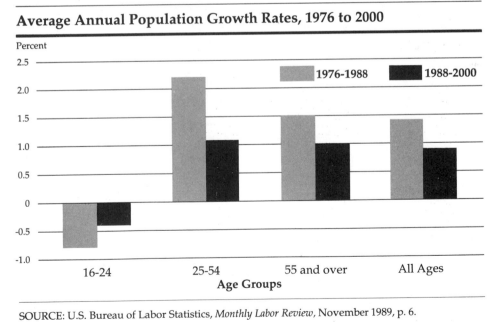

SOURCE: U.S. Bureau of Labor Statistics, *Monthly Labor Review*, November 1989, p. 6.

demographic assumptions involving high rates of fertility, mortality, and immigration. The high-dependency scenario emerges from an alternative set of assumptions involving lower rates of these same demographic trends. The ratio of older to working-age people will be rising under any assumption, although the size of the increase will be greatly affected by future trends in births, deaths, and immigration. If birth, death, and immigration rates are low, the ratio of older workers to those of working age will be nearly three times as high in 2050 as it is today.

Births are a key variable. The U.S. birthrate is much lower today than it was after World War II. It has hovered around 1.8 children per woman, which is below a *replacement* fertility rate of 2.1. Our rate is slightly above that of many other industrialized nations (e.g., Germany and Japan) but well below the rate in most developing countries.

The work force of the 1990s will also be more diverse. Labor force growth rates for blacks, Hispanics, and Asians will greatly exceed those for whites, and the growth rate for women will exceed that for men within all races (see Figure 3). Yet, our existing institutions tend to be most experienced in assimilating white males into the work force.

Thus, we are entering an era marked by an aging population and a work force that will grow very slowly and perhaps even shrink in the early part of the next century. Taken together, these trends portend a rising burden on each person of working age because a smaller percentage of the total population will be the breadwinners for the nation. Tomorrow's workers will need to be very productive.

FIGURE 2

Number of Persons 65 Years of Age or Older for Each 100 Persons Age 20 to 64

	Low-Dependency Scenario	High-Dependency Scenario
1990	21	21
2010	21	24
2030	33	45
2050	30	59

SOURCE: U.S. Bureau of the Census, Current Population Reports, Series P-25, No. 1057, U.S. Population Estimates by Age, Sex, Race, and Hispanic Origin: 1989, (Washington, D.C.: U.S. Government Printing Office, 1990).

THE NEED FOR NEW APPROACHES

Dramatic population shifts and significant changes in the nature of work are making many of our existing public and private policies and institutions obsolete. If they are to serve the long-term interest of a more diverse America, major changes are needed.

The U.S. economy and work force have adjusted well to many important changes in the past. We have undergone a steady long-run shift of workers from agricultural to industrial jobs. The share of our labor force in manufacturing jobs has declined steadily as more new jobs have been created in the service sector.

But the new demographic challenge is even more formidable, and it will affect all sectors of the economy. For example, it is often said that a good education is increasingly important for workers performing service-sector jobs. Yet, a person cannot work in a factory today without a solid basic education, computer data entry skills, an ability to read and decipher manuals, and an understanding of how to organize and process information.

In this world of *electronic immigration*, where work can be done on one continent and faxed to another in minutes, U.S. workers are competing

FIGURE 3

Average Annual Labor Force Growth Rates Among Various Demographic Groups, 1988 to 2000

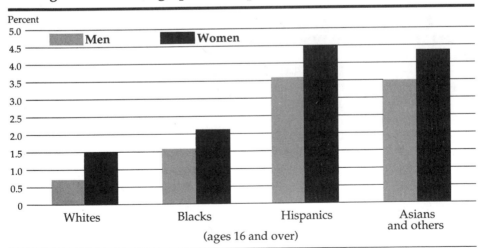

Note: Hispanics may be of any race; the Asians and others group includes American Indians, Alaskan natives, Asians, and Pacific Islanders.

SOURCE: U.S. Bureau of Labor Statistics, *Monthly Labor Review*, November 1989, p. 8.

with other workers worldwide to fill the rapidly upgraded requirements of today's economy.

We are moving toward an economy in which information and knowledge are critical, basic skills in reading comprehension and mathematics are vital, and social and interpersonal abilities are necessary. Yet, there is already a gap between what we need and what we have in these areas, and the gap will widen under business-as-usual practices. These developments could add up to a major competitive handicap for American business, a deplorable waste of our human resources, and a human tragedy for the millions of individuals who will be unable to benefit from a useful and rewarding working career.

International demographic trends also cause concern. The work forces of Africa, Asia, and Latin America will grow by about 1 billion over the next twenty years. Mexico alone will add about 1 million people a year to its work force during the 1990s; and even with 3 percent-a-year real growth in GNP, it would have nearly 20 percent of its work force unemployed in the year 2000. Insufficient jobs for young workers in their homelands could create serious pressure for emigration, especially to the United States.

In sum, these trends, if left unattended, could precipitate a succession of increasingly painful economic and social crises because the U.S. work force would lack the size and skills needed to sustain economic growth. We have an interval of time, a window of opportunity, to adjust and possibly to turn some of these changes into advantages. The question is whether we have the wisdom and the will to do so.

THE LIFE-CYCLE APPROACH

Public policy often tends to segment problems artificially by age group or subject matter. But the goal of creating a stronger, more competitive work force calls for a dramatically different approach.

The life-cycle view we present in this policy statement links each stage of life and work to the next and takes into account the interrelated nature of needs and problems. Youths will one day be adults, and adults will grow old. Within this framework, public and private policies should aim at:

- Preparing youths for rewarding working lives and for participation in mainstream community life

- Helping adults to be self-sufficient and socially responsible through productive work and skill renewal and to make some provision for their own retirement needs through saving and insurance

- Keeping older citizens active and independent

Public policies that affect the work force need to be integrated across the life cycle. For example, instead of attacking health care problems piecemeal, through fragmented and unconnected policies that simply shift costs from one group to another, we should pursue *comprehensive* reforms. The same approach is needed in education, job training, retirement, and other policies that affect the work force.

People are living longer, and their needs vary at different times in life. Therefore, we also need to develop better policy connections from one stage of life to another. This is the essence of the life-cycle approach.

Where is it written that everyone must work eight hours a day, fifty weeks a year, for forty years and then stop work abruptly at age 65? We need to rethink the conventional categories of work and nonwork and the organization of working time. Instead of rigid delineation, we need to foster flexible arrangements that may, for example, accommodate the needs of older workers or parents with young children.

Instead of sharp breaks between work and retirement, we need to develop new opportunities for older workers to phase down their work effort gradually and remain employed on less than a full-time basis, if suitable. We also need to recognize how nonmarket work – caring for family and civic activities – supports rather than competes with paid employment.

To deal with increased longevity, individuals need to – and need to be helped to – prepare for both a long work life and a long retirement period. The fact that many people will need extra care as they get older must be dealt with squarely, and this makes the productivity of those still working even more important.

Clearly, the demographic trends we describe in this statement hold the potential for creating real generational conflict. To the extent that our conceptual framework leads to policies that bring social benefits across generations, we can help avert this conflict.

By redefining mutual interests, obligations, and relationships in these new circumstances, for both individuals and society, the life-cycle approach can provide the vision of a new intergenerational compact and the practical framework for constructing it, to help bind generations together rather than divide them.

For example, policies that help older people remain active and independent are not just beneficial to the elderly. They also help relieve succeeding generations of the economic pressure of dependency in old age. One of the striking findings of our study is how much the favorable effects of policies in any one stage of the life-cycle promise to be enhanced by the effectiveness of good policies in the other phases.

INVESTING IN CHILDREN AND YOUTH

Investing wisely in our nation's most precious resource, our children, is the start of the life-cycle approach. Yet, some sobering facts and trends show how far we have to go.

- One of five children under age 18 today lives in poverty.

- The U.S. infant mortality rate exceeds that of most other industrial countries and remains about twice as high for blacks as for whites.

- Fewer than one in five children in lower-income households is enrolled in a preschool program.

- About 15 percent of all youths and about 40 percent of Hispanic youths never complete high school.

- A substantial portion of those who do complete high school cannot perform simple mental tasks or organize and process information.

- About 1 million teenage girls get pregnant each year; and although the overall teenage pregnancy rate has edged downward, pregnancies among unmarried teenage girls constitute a much higher proportion of this total.

- The rate of college enrollment has dropped among minority young people.

National efforts must begin with an effort to prevent premature parenthood among teenagers. It is equally important to improve the odds that babies will be born healthy by providing adequate and timely prenatal care. We must then make a major effort to foster universally sound childhood development policies, including high-quality child care and broader participation in programs such as Head Start. **We urge full funding of Head Start for every eligible child.**

In our 1987 policy statement *Children in Need: Investment Strategies for the Educationally Disadvantaged*, CED recognized the importance to the economy of the earliest years of life. A 1985 policy statement, *Investing in Our Children: Business and the Public Schools*, highlighted the need to make major changes in our elementary and secondary education system to improve its performance.

In this statement, we stress the importance of developing and implementing major systemic reforms in our elementary and secondary education system to improve educational attainment, achieve basic literacy, and enable all children to learn how to learn. We focus on the need to lower the dropout rate, increase college enrollment (particularly for minority groups), and smooth the transition from school to work. We believe that all areas of education reform require the active involvement of parents, educators, and business and community leaders.

We support the effort of the President and the governors to develop national goals for education. Beyond that, we need nationally accepted measures of performance and strategies for reaching our goals. Setting goals and devising strategies for meeting them should also be the responsibility of states, local schools districts, and individual schools.

We believe that permitting parents and students to choose among competing public schools and programs has the potential to improve public school performance, but only if implemented as part of a broad strategy of restructuring. Restructuring could include improvements in the curriculum, a better organization of the school day, and pay systems that reward good performance by teachers. The essential feature of educational reform is to hold all players in the system accountable for better student outcomes.

WHAT BUSINESS CAN DO. Because of its resources and influence in the community, we call on business to help attain these goals and to provide the support that schools need to fulfill their mission. This may include lending talent to the school system, providing part-time and summer work experiences, setting clear hiring standards that are communicated to schools, and entering into reciprocal agreements with schools in which concrete job commitments are linked to improved educational outcomes.

But perhaps **the most important role business can play is as advocate both for children and for quality education.** At a time when parents with children in public schools make up a minority of the nation's voters, business' sustained involvement in promoting quality education for all children can be a powerful and persuasive force.

Business needs to be more precise in its identification of employability skills and it needs to develop a close and continuing relationship with educators in order to define education goals that are compatible with those skills.

INTEGRATED INTERVENTION STRATEGIES. The picture is not all bleak. Viewed as a whole, the current generation of young people faces better prospects and enjoys a higher standard of living than previous generations. Labor market conditions during the 1990s will favor new entrants, but only those with adequate skills and abilities. This will present an opportunity to narrow the gaps between minority and nonminority workers.

But a substantial proportion of young people is ill-equipped to take advantage of those opportunities even under the most favorable labor market conditions because of inadequate basic skills, alcohol and drug abuse, teen parenthood, and welfare dependency. Often, these same young people are struggling with many of these problems at once. The combined efforts of the public and private sectors, rather than piecemeal efforts, are needed to give them the support they need to participate in our economy and become self-sufficient.

These efforts hold the potential to provide a double-barrel benefit: youths who turn away from a life of dependency and instead become productive workers will pay more taxes and draw down fewer benefits. This will help us stretch our limited public resources to meet the needs of people who cannot work and must rely on public support.

It is therefore critical to weave the often loose strands of services and support into a more coherent program. **We need to make services to children and families and to the educational system work in concert to assure a smooth transition and continual flow of support from infancy into adulthood.**

HELPING THE CURRENT WORKER ADJUST

As America's work force matures and the core of experienced workers entering their forties and fifties expands, U.S. productivity should receive a boost. But the combination of outdated job skills, a growing reluctance to go where the jobs are, and widespread vested nonportable pension benefits may reduce flexibility. With the smaller "baby bust" generation trailing behind baby boomers, America faces a two-pronged challenge: to make the smaller cohort of new workers as well educated and trained as possible and to help the larger group of existing workers adjust to changing circumstances.

FROM SCHOOL TO WORK. One of the weak links in the American system of human capital investment is the connection between school and work. In contrast with their peers abroad, American high school students frequently do not have good job skills and are left to fend for themselves in the job market. These inadequacies are reflected in the fact that between 1973 and 1986, the real earnings of American high school students who did not go to college dropped by 28 percent.

Those students heading directly into the work force from high school often need help with the transition. **Programs that target high school students before major problems set in, such as Jobs for America's Graduates, can be very effective in getting young people back on track, as can** vocational programs that combine work force skills with solid academic training.

More attention needs to be paid to retrieving dropouts through the use of alternative schools and entrepreneurial education and through such proven residential programs as the Job Corps, which deserves additional funding in order to reach more of its target population.

To foster greater postsecondary education and training, business and government should consider alternative approaches such as tax credits or vouchers under a postsecondary "GI bill."

EMPLOYEE EDUCATION. As a natural complement to revitalizing our education system, we need to improve the learning that takes place on the job.

As the speed of change in the workplace accelerates, more training and retraining will be required. Workers increasingly will need more advanced skills just to qualify for the kinds of training that will be given. It may have once been possible to pay high wages to low-skilled workers, but it will be exceedingly difficult to do so in the future. We believe that more and more firms will be budgeting for education and training just as they do for investments in physical capital.

Changes in U.S. tax policies could stimulate new investment in employee education and development. But current tax policies do not favor such investments. A federal tax credit for training and new state policies to encourage individuals to invest in themselves could recoup their costs in the form of taxes paid on increased individual and corporate earnings.

PAY AND BENEFITS. To boost productivity, pay practices need to reward performance more and seniority less. Flexible compensation plans with positive incentives for performance should be more widely used.

Business and labor will need to work more cooperatively on such issues as holding down health care costs, moderating wage increases, and relaxing restrictive work rules in return for added job security. Business can take the lead in health care by creating strong incentives to control the cost of health benefits and placing the proper emphasis on preventive care. Individual responsibility also needs to be stressed in obtaining treatment for alcohol and drug abuse as well as other personal problems. Smaller and medium-sized businesses need to develop new ways to pool risks and offer affordable health insurance to the many uninsured workers and their dependents.

FAMILY POLICIES. To respond to the needs of workers with family obligations and to increase the pool of workers, employers should fashion employee scheduling and leave policies that suit the needs of their own business and work force *before* such policies become mandated by law. Business may also find that such forward-looking family policies are powerful recruiting and retention tools.

In the case of child care, employer policies should be tailored to meet the needs of their employees and the company, offering a range of choices that might include direct provision of services, referral to community-based child care, direct subsidization of such services, or allowing employees to shelter a part of their income under a dependent-care plan.

Government child-care policy needs to target child-care assistance more closely to financial need. **We recommend capping the child and dependent care tax credit and using the revenue to help low-income families.**

In any case, primary responsibility for selecting and financing child care must rest with parents, and neither employers nor government should preempt parents as decision makers. Many workers also need to care for aging relatives, and new policies and practices are needed to address these responsibilities.

We urge employers to institute their own family-leave policies, suited to their own circumstances. We understand, but do not endorse, legislatively mandated approaches to family leave, which impose arbitrary and costly requirements on business.

BROADENING THE WORK FORCE POOL. Another important element in expanding the pool of workers is making full utilization of the talents and energies of people with disabilities. An estimated 40 million Americans are disabled to some extent, and about one-third of them are working full-time. Many are too young, too old, or too disabled to work, but many others want to work and face stiff obstacles.

Business can help by redesigning jobs to fit the special circumstances of people with disabilities and by recognizing their excellent work records. This can often be accomplished at little or no cost.

Government policies toward disability also need to be reformed. There is currently too much emphasis on income maintenance and too little attention to rehabilitation. The *medical model* of intervention, focusing exclusively on the role of doctors, hospitals, and medicine, is overstressed to the detriment of needed social services and the importance of independent living.

For workers dislocated by economic change, a few months of unemployment benefits will not solve their problem. Unfortunately, the unemployment insurance system offers little help to someone seeking new skills or a new career. **We recommend that a significant amount of unemployment insurance funds be earmarked for retraining and relocation of workers.**

In this policy statement, we also highlight strategies to bring welfare recipients into the labor force. Some elements of this strategy include augmenting the income of the working poor to assure that full-time work lifts people out of poverty and altering our welfare system to reduce dependency and foster work. **The earned-income tax credit should be increased to make work more rewarding for low-income Americans.**

We emphasize initiatives that enable workers to help themselves, not paternalistic efforts by business and government and heavy-handed, top-down assistance. We also highlight some promising programs emerging from the nonprofit sector that help instill motivation and positive values while building skills. As these examples demonstrate, there is more to making the transition from welfare to work than the acquisition of skills.

IMMIGRATION. Another way to increase the supply of workers is through immigration policies. We should both increase overall immigration and adjust the mix to reflect new economic and demographic realities. But we should do so in a way that accommodates and supports efforts to bring our nation's hard-to-employ into the work force.*

U.S. immigration policies should not be shaped only by labor market needs; strong consideration should continue to be given to family reunification, humanitarian, foreign policy, and other criteria. But there is a need for more careful and explicit consideration of the labor market effects of immigration.

Increasing immigration to meet the needs of the labor market must not be a substitute for upgrading the skills of the U.S.-born population or for bringing more disadvantaged citizens into the work force. Nor should the very real problems of short-run displacements or local economic and social disruption be ignored.

But, sensitive to those issues, we believe that immigration is a positive contributor to economic growth and that the ratio of permanent immigrants permitted entry under labor market classifications should move gradually from the current 1 to 10 to at least 4 to 10 by 1998.

ACTIVE AND INDEPENDENT OLDER CITIZENS

Both private business practices and public policies discourage work by older people, and we argue for making greater labor force participation more attractive to older workers.

Many private-sector retirement programs encourage early retirement, and U.S. workers, particularly males, are responding. Fully one out of three men ages 60 to 64 is completely out of the work force. Work by those over 65 is limited, although there is evidence that the decline has bottomed

---

*See memoranda by THOMAS J. EYERMAN (page 162).

out and that older Americans work at least as much as or more than older people in other countries. In a changing demographic climate, business needs to reevaluate policies that push older workers out the door. Incentives to retire early may have made sense in a world where jobs were scarce and labor plentiful. As the situation reverses, policies need to be changed.

Labor markets in the 1970s and early 1980s were such that job opportunities for unemployed older workers were often nonexistent or highly unattractive. But the emerging shortage of younger workers and the increasing deficits in skills and knowledge of these workers will improve employment opportunities for older workers in the 1990s.

Social Security discourages work by people 65 to 69 years old, as benefits are reduced if earnings rise above a specified level. Moreover, a 1986 congressional action made employers of Medicare-eligible workers the primary payers of health insurance benefits under company health plans. This can be a deterrent to an employer to hire or retain an older Medicare-eligible employee.

Our society fails to offer enough diversity in employment alternatives to older Americans. Many older people will not want full-time paid employment, but this does not mean that they wish to be idle. Accordingly, we recommend the following changes in public and private policies to retain and recruit more older Americans to the work force:

- **Remove the earned-income test for Social Security payments after age 65 and make this revenue-neutral by including a larger share of Social Security benefits in taxable income.**

- **Experiment with ways in which the federal government, employers, and unions can jointly manage Medicare and retiree health benefits.**

- **Restructure pension plans that penalize workers for staying beyond normal retirement age.**

- **Offer older workers flexible working conditions, possibly through benefit packages that allow workers to "buy" additional weeks of vacation or leave or by allowing reduced hours without reduced status or pay level.**

- **Allow companies more flexibility in moving dollars from over-funded pension plans to underfunded retiree health plans.**

- **Place more emphasis on preventing disability and helping disabled employees return to work.**

The key to public and private policies regarding older workers is moving away from the all-or-nothing approach and making creative changes in employment, retirement, and benefit policies that will encourage those older Americans who can to participate in a productive economy.

In addition to encouraging work among the "young old," we need to find ways to keep the "old old" as active and independent as possible. This will require a much greater role for the private voluntary sector in assisting the frail elderly with the activities of daily living. It will also require a reexamination of our private and social insurance programs to protect Americans against the financial risks of long-term care.

FINANCING THE TRANSITION

Fundamentally, we are calling for a new way of thinking about and acting on a wide variety of economic and social issues that will determine the quality of the American work force. Our goal is to design policies and programs that will help Americans develop and utilize fully the skills and talents that will keep our country strong and productive.

Some of our recommendations call on business, labor, and government to recognize the need for new investments in human resources. We provide some illustrations of the likely costs of such investments, as well as the return we believe these investments will yield. Individuals will also have to invest in themselves to prepare for changing circumstances. And a number of our recommendations envision the restructuring of government programs at the federal, state, or local levels. Some of these recommendations for public-sector action call for new government spending.

We recognize that new public-sector commitments must be fully financed. With the proper discipline, we can afford carefully targeted new spending even as we set about the vital task of reducing the federal budget deficit. We believe that a financing package for new federal initiatives should follow the important guidelines that CED set forth in its 1989 statement *Battling America's Budget Deficit*.

To the extent possible, **financing should come from putting credible and lasting restraints on spending for a wide range of government programs, including major entitlement programs and national defense.** If and when national defense spending is substantially reduced, this too could be considered to help fund some of these programs.

Budget cuts should be real, not illusory, and should not be made by whacking away at means-tested entitlement programs. However, such programs can be redesigned to increase their efficiency. And any tax increases that form a part of a financing package should be designed so as not to deter private saving or productive investment.

Even recommendations that will entail costs are for the most part *investments* – **investments that will pay back most of their original cost and**

frequently more than that amount. For example, we recommend that Head Start be funded to serve every eligible child (instead of the 20 percent currently enrolled). The up-front cost of enrolling all eligible children would be about $5 to $6 billion more than we currently spend. But solid research has shown that for every dollar invested in quality preschool child development, society is paid back $6 in the form of increased taxes eventually paid by these children and lower costs of special education, public assistance, and crime.

Appendix A summarizes the evidence on the cost-effectiveness of investments in Head Start and a variety of other early-intervention efforts, including Medicaid and the Special Supplemental Food Program for Women, Infants, and Children (WIC).

CED'S APPROACH

This policy statement traces the dimensions of emerging population changes and considers their implications for the workplace. It builds a case for investing in human capital throughout an individual's life, beginning with prenatal care and early-childhood development and extending to more productive use of older workers and greater security for retirees. Our life-cycle approach to human resources recognizes that investments made at earlier stages of life pay dividends at later stages and that policies helping older workers readjust to changing circumstances help younger workers as well.

The changing demographic context requires us to pay more attention to increasing the proportion of our potential labor force that is actually employed and to enhancing the productivity of all workers. These forces also impel us to reexamine our immigration policies.

In our view, improving the productivity of the U.S.-born population and placing greater emphasis on economic considerations in our immigration policies are two basic components of a comprehensive approach to averting labor shortages that could constrain economic growth.

As the ratio of working-age people to retirees declines in the years ahead, we will need to recruit as many potential workers as possible. This requires us to identify the sources of underutilized labor and to devise strategies for drawing people into productive endeavors. It also requires us to identify and overcome the barriers to employment that face some potential workers.

In the chapters that follow, we detail a two-pronged approach: first, to make the existing work force more productive and flexible and, second, to augment the size of that work force by creating opportunities for underutilized groups of potential workers. These groups include parents with child-care responsibilities, people with limited education and training, people with health problems and disabilities, older workers who might otherwise retire, immigrants, and those working in the underground economy.

* * *

Faced with slowing population growth, we must move quickly to develop our human resources into a smarter, more productive work force that can sustain economic growth. To do this, we must close the troubling gap between the higher skill levels required in the new job market and the lower skills possessed by many new labor force entrants. Closing this gap will require that we adopt a life-cycle learning process transcending age boundaries and that we help workers adjust to changing circumstances.

Meeting this challenge will entail costs, and this policy statement examines some of those costs. Avoiding this challenge, however, will be far more costly. This statement is meant to serve as a call for change in public policies and business practices in response to the enormous social, economic, and cultural changes that challenge us on every front.

Chapter 2

Demographic Trends

A brief summary of some key facts and trends indicates the dimensions of demographic changes taking place in this country.

The size of the working-age population will grow more slowly.

- Labor force growth, which averaged 2.9 percent a year in the 1970s, is expected to average only 1 percent in the 1990s. In the early part of the next century, the size of the labor force will flatten out and, according to some projections, actually decline slightly.

- The slow growth of the working-age population will cause labor markets to tighten. It will put a premium on utilizing the potential of everyone in the working-age years and helping them to be active and productive.

The composition of the working-age population is changing dramatically. In addition to the changes in the size of the work force and the retiree population, there are important changes in the *mix* of the work force.

MEN

- Between 1948 and 1987, the proportion of men over age 65 who were working dropped from 46.8 percent to 16.3 percent. According to the U.S. Bureau of Labor Statistics (BLS), the labor force participation rate of men 55 years of age and older fell from 47.8 percent in 1976 to 39.9 percent in 1988. The Bureau projects that this rate will slip a little further to 38.9 percent in 2000.[1] (See Figure 4.)

- In 1987, two out of three male workers eligible for Social Security benefits retired before age 65 despite the permanently reduced benefit; three of four female workers chose early retirement.

WOMEN

- More women are working for pay. BLS data show that 72.7 percent of women between the ages of 25 and 54 were working in 1988, an increase from 33.6 percent in 1947. The bureau projects a labor force participation rate of 81.4 percent for this group in 2000. About 56 percent of women with children under six years old were working in 1988. The labor force participation rate of older women was stable from the mid-1970s to the mid-1980s and then increased significantly in the 1985-1988 period. Projections for the decade ahead show slight increases.[2]

FIGURE 4

Labor Force Participation Rates of Older Men and Adult Women,* 1964 to 2000

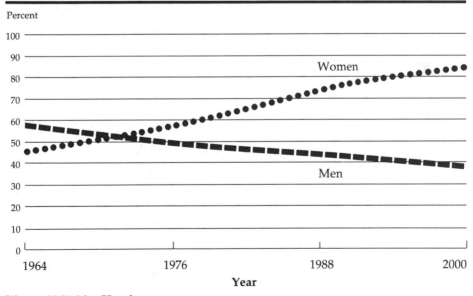

*Women 25-54, Men 55 and over.

SOURCE: U.S. Department of Labor, Bureau of Labor Statistics, *Monthly Labor Review*, November 1989, p. 5.

- Women make up an increasing proportion of the labor force. They accounted for 45 percent of the labor force in 1988, compared with 38.1 percent in 1970 and 29.6 percent in 1950. The BLS projection for 2000 shows women making up 47 percent, or nearly half, of the work force. Moreover, about 62 percent of the net growth in the work force between 1988 and 2000 will be accounted for by women, according to bureau projections.[3]

A number of trends have been converging to bring about this dramatic long-term change in female labor force participation. First, there are more single women and women without children up to the age of about 35, and work is an obvious option for them. Second, there has been a sharp growth of single-parent families headed by women, and most must work. Third, there has been a large increase in the proportion of married women with children who work, reflecting both changing attitudes about the role of women and economic necessity associated with the stagnation in real earnings among males in their prime-age working years.

Moreover, although progress has been slow, women are beginning to penetrate traditionally male-dominated professional and technical occupations.

In several important ways, these trends have eroded the traditional stereotype of the male head of household as the sole breadwinner. Cultural and attitudinal changes have interacted with economic necessity to blur the earlier image of male dominance and clear-cut gender distinctions in the labor force.

MINORITIES

Minorities are also becoming a more important part of the U.S. labor force. Blacks and Hispanics, who together made up 18 percent of the U.S. population in 1988, are projected to account for 22 percent in 2000.[4] And if current fertility patterns continue, blacks and Hispanics could constitute 35 percent of the work force in 2020. The non-Hispanic white majority in the United States will eventually become a minority,[5] and the majority-minority distinction will be replaced by various pluralities, varying from region to region.

A significant proportion of expected net growth in the labor force between 1988 and 2000 (27.4 percent) will be accounted for by Hispanics (most of whom are white). Blacks' contribution to net labor force growth is projected to be 15.7 percent in this period. The corresponding figure for Asians is 9.6 percent.[6] Thus, these three groups together will account for more than half of net labor force growth during the 1988-2000 period, according to BLS projections.

FIGURE 5

Trends Affecting Black Youths

	Gains	
	1968	1985
Median years of school completed	9	12
Proportion of 20- to 24-year-olds who had finished high school	57.6%	80.8%
Black income as a percentage of white income among two-earner families	73%	85%
	Losses	
	1973	1986
Real median income of families headed by persons 24 years old or younger (1986 dollars)	$11,997	$6,400
	1974	1986
Marriage rates of 20- to 24-year-old males who did not complete high school	24.4%	7.9%
	1968	1987
Percentage of men employed	70%	56%

SOURCES: R. Scott Fosler, "The Political and Institutional Implications of Demographic Change," Vol. IV of the Committee for Economic Development's Project on the Policy Implications of Demographic Change, Washington, D.C., April 1988; U.S. Department of Labor, *Monthly Labor Review*, November 1989; and *The Forgotten Half: Pathways to Success for America's Youth and Young Families*, Youth and America's Future: the William T. Grant Commission on Work, Family, and Citizenship, Washington, D.C. 1989.

For a number of reasons, many more blacks and Hispanics than whites have reached working age in our society in conditions that handicap their productive employment. Evidence suggests that those handicaps are becoming less widespread, but they still exist. As a group, blacks have made significant gains in recent years, particularly in the area of educational attainment (see Figure 5). Black families with two adults working have done particularly well.

The problem is that a significant number of adult blacks are either women who are single parents or men who are not in the labor force at all.

FIGURE 6

Actual and Projected Proportions of All Households That Are Married Couples

Year	Married Couples as a Percentage of Households
1970	71%
1980	61
1990	56
2000	53
1986	
Whites	60
Hispanics	57
Blacks	38

SOURCE: U.S. Bureau of the Census, Current Population Reports, Series P-20, No. 441, *Households, Family, Marital Status and Living Arrangements: March 1989* Advance Report, (Washington, D.C.: U.S. Government Printing Office, 1989).

Reflecting the importance of education in the labor market, the real income of 20- to 24- year-old black men with college degrees rose 6.5 percent between 1973 and 1986 while the real earnings of high school dropouts fell 60.6 percent over this period.[7]

As many blacks have escaped the inner-city poverty syndrome by completing school, getting married, relocating to the suburbs, and obtaining jobs, the inner cities of America have become centers of highly concentrated poverty with very high incidences of female-headed black families, teenage pregnancy, failure to complete school, long-term welfare dependency, and weak attachment to the labor force.

With about 43 percent of black children under 18 years old living in poverty and a majority living in a household headed by a female with no father present, a challenging issue for the future is the difficult odds that many of today's black youths will face in becoming self-sufficient and productive members of the labor force tomorrow.

These trends, of course, are not limited to blacks. For example, the proportion of teenage births that are out of wedlock has climbed sharply among both blacks and whites, and the married-couple household is on the decline across the board (see Figure 6). Moreover, Hispanics have a much higher high school dropout rate (about 40 percent) than whites or blacks and have experienced an erosion of earnings since the early 1970s.

IMMIGRANTS

Immigrants are also accounting for a larger share of the U.S. population and will become a more important part of the labor force in the future.

- Legal immigration is estimated at about 6 million for the 1980s, nearly double the inflow of legal immigrants in the 1960s (see Figure 7). Immigrants are expected to account for almost one-fourth of the labor force growth between 1985 and 2000.

An estimated 3.3 million legal immigrants entered the United States in the 1960s, about 34 percent of whom were from Europe (about 90 percent of immigrants in the nineteenth century were from Europe). This flow rose to 4.5 million in the 1970s, but the proportion from Europe was cut to 18 percent. The figures for the 1980s are volatile, reaching a peak of 845,000 in 1980 and then appearing to level off in the range of about 600,000 per year in the mid-1980s. A significant proportion of 1980s immigrants were from Latin America and Asia.

In addition to these legal immigrants, there is an unknown number of illegal immigrants. The 1980 census estimated their number at 2.1 million, but many observers believe it is much higher. A challenge that is parallel and equal to that of bringing the nation's indigenous minority population into the mainstream of our economic and social life is to facilitate the full integration of the immigrant population into the work force and society. In an era of tight labor markets, there is no reason why one person's gain has to translate into another person's loss. Helping minorities and helping immigrants (some of whom are minorities themselves) are not antithetical, but rather complementary goals. (Chapter 7 is devoted to the challenge of utilizing the skills of immigrants in the labor market.)

OLDER CITIZENS

The size of the non-working elderly population is growing more rapidly.

- The ratio of older to working-age Americans will depend on fertility, immigration, and mortality rates. The higher these rates are, the lower the dependency ratio of older to working-age Americans will be. In 1988, there were 21 persons 65 and older for every 100 persons age

FIGURE 7

Trends in Legal Immigration

Decades	Number of Immigrants (in millions)	Percentage from Europe
1960s	3.3	34%
1970s	4.5	18
1980s (estimate)	6.0	17

SOURCE: *1988 Statistical Yearbook*, Immigration and Naturalization Service, Tables 1 and 2, (Washington, D.C.: U.S. Government Printing Office, 1989).

20 to 64. In 2050, there could be anywhere from 30 to 59 persons 65 and older for every 100 persons age 20 to 64, depending on whether fertility, immigration, and mortality rates produce a low- or a high-dependency situation.

- Irrespective of whether a low- or high-dependency scenario unfolds, there will inevitably be a sharply increasing number of older persons relative to the working-age population (see Figure 8).

- Although different fertility, immigration, and mortality assumptions can change the projections for Social Security and Medicare expenditures, the performance of the economy will be just as important to the relative financial burden that the working

FIGURE 8

Number of Persons 65 Years of Age and Older Per 100 Persons Age 20 to 64, 1988-2050

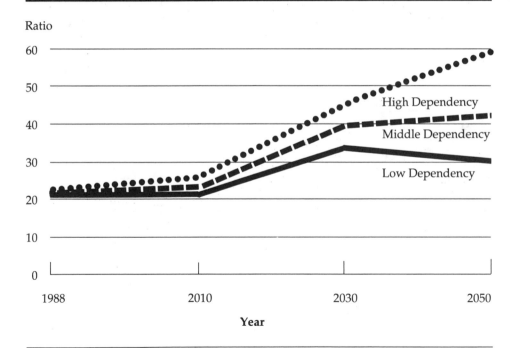

SOURCE: U.S. Bureau of the Census, Current Population Reports, Series P-25, No. 1018, *Projections of the Population of the U.S. by Age, Sex, and Race: 1988-2080*, (Washington, D.C.: U.S. Government Printing Office, 1990).

population will bear for financing entitlements for older persons. High employment, gains in productivity, low inflation, and other favorable economic trends would reduce the relative burden on the workers. Alternatively, high unemployment, poor productivity growth, and high inflation would exacerbate the demographics-induced burdens on the working-age population. Thus, the impact of demographics, although important, should be viewed in a larger economic context.

The needs of the non-working aged will increase faster than their numbers. In addition to the growth in the elderly population, the elderly themselves will be aging. The fastest-growing subgroup is comprised of those 85 years old and over. They account for 1 percent of the population today but will grow to about 5 percent in the middle of the next century (from 2.5 million to 16 million people). This rapidly growing group is about 10 times as likely to need assistance with daily living as those 65 to 69 years old. Also, the United States lacks a social insurance system, public or private, that spreads the risks associated with long-term care for the elderly. Families face the possibility of impoverishment from the costs of chronic illness and disability that force them to "spend down."

- The aging of the U.S. population will be putting pressure on our public and private systems of retirement and health benefits. For example, Medicare's Hospital Insurance Trust Fund is expected to run out of money in the early part of the next century if something is not done about rising health costs (see Figure 9). Many companies face sharp negative adjustments in their balance sheets because the application of financial accounting standards to the funding of retiree health benefits reflects the current value of future company obligations. Workers face high levels of payroll taxes to finance Social Security and Medicare benefits for a swelling elderly population.

Some of the working-age population will be dependent, too. A significant segment of the working-age population is living in families with incomes below poverty and not working. Children growing up in poverty today will find it harder to be self-sufficient tomorrow. Many working families lack financial protection against the advent of illness, disability, unemployment, and old age. Not only are they unable to support themselves when these events occur but they also are unable to share the responsibility with their working peers to support the growing elderly population.

RESERVOIR OF POTENTIAL WORKERS

Although immigration can help to meet the demand for workers in a tightening labor market, we should not overlook the reservoir of potential workers who are not in the labor force. There are 62.5 million people over age 16 who are not in the labor force (see Figure 10). The vast majority of these persons do not wish to be employed for various reasons. For example, about 24 million of them have family and household responsibilities, nearly 18 million are retired, 6 million are in school, and almost 5 million are disabled or in ill health.

FIGURE 9

Hospital Insurance Trust Fund Balance

Balance in Billions of Dollars

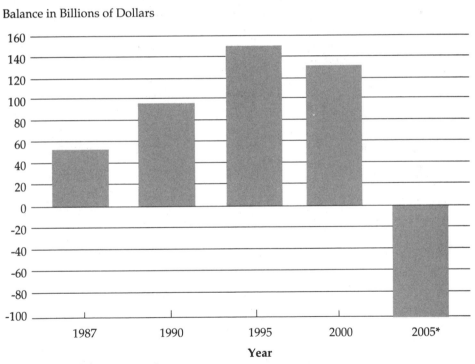

Year

*Magnitude of deficit is uncertain.

SOURCE: *1989 Annual Report of the Board of Trustees of the Federal Hospital Insurance Trust Fund*, U.S. Department of Health and Human Services (Washington, D.C.: U.S. Government Printing Office 1989).

There are, however, 5.4 million people who are not in the labor force but who indicate that they want to work. About 1.4 million are in school, 1.2 million have family responsibilities, 925,000 are disabled or in ill health, and 859,000 are discouraged workers, who believe that they do not have sufficient skills or that there are no suitable jobs available.

FIGURE 10

Reservoir of Persons Over Age 16 Not in the Labor Force (annual averages, 1989)

Persons not wanting a job	**57,129,000**
Primary reason:	
Disabled/ill health	**4,731,000**
In school	**6,423,000**
Family and household responsibilities	**24,046,000**
Retirement	**17,791,000**
Age 55-59	**334,000**
Age 60-64	**2,545,000**
Age 65 or older	**14,785,000**
All others	**4,138,000**
Persons wanting a job	**5,396,000**
Disabled/ill health	**925,000**
In school	**1,355,000**
Family and household responsibilities	**1,219,000**
Discouraged workers	**859,000**
All others	**1,038,000**
Total persons not in the labor force	**62,525,000**

SOURCE: U.S. Department of Labor, Bureau of Labor Statistics, unpublished data from the *Current Population Survey.*

The second group of persons in the reservoir of potential workers is made up of those who have been unemployed for a relatively long period. In 1989, the average level of unemployment at a given time was 5.3 percent, or 6.5 million people. The vast majority of the unemployed are in transition between jobs, but there is a residual group of 600,000 workers who are unemployed for more than twenty-six weeks. Reasons for long-term unemployment include lack of skills, local economic transitions, and the lack of certain prerequisites for working, such as child care or transportation.

The growing demand for part-time and temporary work offers a bridge for some people in the reservoir of potential workers to be employed as an interim step to full-time participation in the labor force.

POVERTY AND WELFARE DEPENDENCY

About 32 million Americans have incomes below the federally determined poverty level. The poverty rate of nonelderly Americans is higher today than it was a decade ago.

About 5 million people work full time at least part of the year but have household incomes below the federal government's poverty line. About 2 million people are poor even though there is a household head working full time throughout the year. When their dependents are counted, an estimated 6 million people live in poverty despite the presence of a full-time, full-year wage earner in the household.

More than 30 million people lack health insurance coverage in the United States; about a third of this group is also living in poverty.

Although the number of people on welfare has not grown for society as a whole, more teenage mothers are becoming welfare recipients. In the late 1970s, about 25 percent of all 15- to 19-year-old teen mothers were recipients. By 1984, about 30 percent were on welfare. If we examine the incidence of welfare dependency during the first four years after a teen mother gives birth, about three-fourths of all teen mothers receive welfare at some point.

DISABILITY

In addition to those living in poverty, many of whom are either out of the labor force altogether or on its margins, the disabled population also contains a sizable group of people who are out of the labor force but could be working and independent. Many of these working-age Americans who are disabled are willing and eager to work but face unnecessary barriers to employment.

- The Social Security Administration reported that as of 1981, there were 22 million persons between the ages of 18 and 64 who were disabled to some extent, one-half of them severely. Of those not severely disabled, 5 million were able to work but not at the same job they were doing prior to disability, whereas 6 million had secondary limitations that restricted them in performing their usual job.[8] This amounts to more than 8.5 percent of the working-age population.[9]

Of those who are working, many are hampered by a lack of basic literacy. Failure to complete high school and illiteracy close the doors to many labor force opportunities; moreover, they hamper the necessary adjustments and transitions that workers must often make in the job market.

- Of the 3.8 million 18-year-olds in 1988, 700,000 had dropped out of high school, and another 700,000 could not read their high school diplomas.

- Nearly 13 percent of all 17-year-olds still enrolled in school are functionally illiterate, and 44 percent are marginally literate.[10]

- In a study conducted for the National Geographic Society, 14 percent of those surveyed could not identify the United States on a world map. This figure is equivalent to 24 million adults. Another 44 million could not identify the Soviet Union or the Pacific Ocean.[11]

- In the same study, only 57 percent of Americans could identify England on a map of Europe.[12]

THE GROWTH OF PART-TIME AND TEMPORARY WORKERS

A combination of demographic and economic trends is leading to the development of a core group of full-time permanent workers supplemented by part-time, temporary, and contract workers. These trends are being intensified by the competitive pressure facing many firms operating in world markets. This ongoing pressure, combined with the need to trim work forces during the severe 1982 recession and the huge appreciation of the dollar during the 1982-1985 period, left many firms with a leaner permanent work force. They have remained more reluctant than in the past to add full-time workers when conditions changed.

The increase in part-time and temporary work is not associated with a disappearance of full-time work or of the middle class, as is often asserted. Nor does it simply reflect pressures from the demand side of the labor market. It also reflects the changing demographics of the work force and the needs of many workers.

- Between December 1983 and December 1987, part-time employment rose by 1 million, or 5.3 percent, while full-time employment increased by 11.8 percent, or 9.9 million people.

- About three of four people working part time (an estimated 15 million people) are doing so voluntarily and do not seek full-time work.

Part-time employment, which now accounts for about one job in six, and temporary work, which now employs several million people who pass through about 800,000 job slots in a year's time, can be a stepping-stone to full-time, permanent work. In addition, part-time and temporary jobs are attractive alternatives for students and older people. Thus, the movement toward more part-time and temporary workers reflects both business needs and worker desires. Although a large part of this work is voluntary, another part reflects the underemployment of those who would rather hold full-time, permanent work.

In addition to facing tough competition from abroad, many firms face takeover threats; as a result, they are more serious than ever about weeding out waste and cutting excess costs. This has led to job termination not only among the rank-and-file work force but also throughout middle management and within the top levels of management. The "restructuring" often needed to keep a firm competitive or to fend off an unfriendly advance has uprooted workers in many sectors of the economy. At the same time, workers have become less likely to remain with one firm and often seek advancement by making job changes or by retooling their skills and moving to different kinds of jobs or other industries.

There is also enough regional diversity in labor markets to make it misleading to talk about "the labor market" in national terms. For example, the national unemployment rate, which stood at 5.2 percent in August 1989, masks a range from 7.4 percent in West Virginia and 7.6 percent in Alabama to as low as 3.1 percent in Nebraska and 3 percent in Virginia. Similarly, the unemployment rate in September 1989 was as high as 8.5 percent in the mining industry and as low as 4.7 percent in transportation and public utilities and 4.5 percent in finance and service industries.[13]

It is important to note that the types of problems highlighted in this chapter – poverty, a lack of educational attainment, failure to complete school, teenage pregnancy, and so on – are not uniformly distributed throughout the country. They are concentrated in inner cities and in certain underdeveloped regions such as the Mississippi Delta. Similarly, the challenge of adjusting to a multicultural, ethnically diverse population is particularly keen in certain regions of the country, such as the Southwest and Florida, although it can also be found in a variety of northern cities from New York and Chicago to Lawrence, Massachusetts.

The United States is not alone in facing the effects of a changing age structure. The aging of the population is also occurring in most other industrial countries. Indeed, in Japan, the proportion of the population age 65 and over will roughly double from about 10 percent to 20 percent or more over the next two to three decades.

By contrast, many developing nations have a large and rising child dependency ratio. These countries have average ages that can be as low as half of the U.S. average. These worldwide population trends translate into a growing surplus of labor in less developed countries juxtaposed against steadily tightening labor markets in the United States and other industrial countries. The result is likely to intensify the pressure leading to immigration into the industrialized countries.

All these projections should ring alarm bells for government officials and public-sector leaders. The combination of a stable or slightly shrinking labor force required to support a growing older, nonworking population and skill deficiencies and dependency *within* the working-age population means that the burden on those who are working will be very great. Indeed, under the middle scenario depicted in Figure 8, the ratio of workers to retirees will change from 5:1 now to 5:2 in less than fifty years. Hence, there is a need to reduce dependency and a corresponding need to bolster productivity.

Chapter 3

Investing in Children and Youth

An individual's capacity for productive employment is determined by a variety of factors from the earliest moments of life. The health of the mother who carries the baby; the care and discipline provided to the child by the family and community; the quality of child care, education, and guidance; and the specific preparation for employment – all play a role in shaping an individual's progress in the world of work. As a result, concern about the nation's future work force must inevitably focus on child development and education.

Until now, the multi-dimensional and interrelated nature of factors affecting young people's capability for later success in working life has been largely ignored by public policy. Too often, society has identified a single problem and assumed that its solution would take care of the difficulties associated with work force preparation. As the gap between worker qualifications and work force needs widened during the 1980s, the spotlight of research and public attention shifted from one major problem to the next, such as inadequate public schools, family turbulence, and growing poverty among children.

It is clear that these various problems are not only serious but are also interrelated. For a substantial part of the U.S. population, they reflect a breakdown in the institutions and systems that have a direct impact on child development and education. The various aspects of personal development are interdependent, and they are the joint responsibilities of numerous social institutions: family, community, school, church, government, and the private sector. The consequence of any one institution's failure to carry out its responsibility falls not only on the child and his or her family but also on society more generally in the form of ill-prepared workers and irresponsible citizens.

There are three principal stages of development and education in the preparation of children and young people for productive employment:

- *Early-childhood development*
- *Primary and secondary education*
- *Postsecondary education*

These stages are not discrete; rather, they overlap in numerous ways. They represent segments on a continuum of learning and development that requires guidance, caring, and education from the earliest moments of life.

Nor is the process concerned exclusively with preparing young people for work. Indeed, its principal purpose is to develop the whole person for personal and spiritual pursuits and social and civic relationships, as well as for economic ends. But there is no reason that all these purposes cannot be served simultaneously and in ways that are mutually reinforcing.

Our intent here is not to examine each stage of child development and education in detail. Numerous studies in recent years have done that, including our own policy statements on these topics. A CED Subcommittee on Education and Child Development is also addressing this issue in greater detail. Our purpose here is to place this process in context, to identify priority needs at each stage, to point out the important ways in which these needs are related to one another, and to suggest how various approaches could be integrated to improve the performance of individual elements in the context of the overall system.

EARLY CHILDHOOD DEVELOPMENT AND EDUCATION

In our 1987 policy statement *Children in Need*, CED called for a comprehensive and coordinated approach to education and child development, beginning with the *prevention* of problems that result in high failure rates among the educationally disadvantaged. **Prevention in this context begins by preventing pregnancy in teenagers who are not ready to be parents and early detection and treatment of health problems and immunization against disease for all pregnant women and their infants. Thereafter, early and sustained intervention is the most effective way to ensure that children embark and stay on the road to successful learning.**

It is in the early years that the foundations are laid and enduring attitudes and habits are established that affect learning and performance for an individual's lifetime. With stimulation, caring, and education appropriate to their stage of development, infants and toddlers will develop the interest, curiosity, habit of learning, sense of mastery, interpersonal skills, and confidence in their self-worth that are the essence and foundation of education and competence.

HEALTHY PARENTS AND CHILDREN

The health of children begins with the health of their mothers. Good prenatal and postnatal care is essential if pregnant teenagers and other high-risk mothers are to give birth to healthy babies. **Priority attention should be given to prenatal care for pregnant teenagers and other women without medical insurance who run a high risk of delivering babies with low birthweight, drug addiction, or other disability-inducing conditions.**

Family health care and developmental screening for children, early detection and treatment of health problems and disabilities, and immunization against preventable disease are also needed to assure that children born healthy stay healthy and that children with health problems get the medical attention they need.

EDUCATION FOR PARENTS AND CAREGIVERS

The responsibility for assuring that infants and children are healthy and that they receive nurturing and guidance from the time they are born rests primarily with parents. But many parents need information and support. **Intervention is needed to keep both mothers and fathers suffering economic and emotional stress from abusing or neglecting their children, and parenting education is needed to help them learn how to nurture their children and become their children's first and best teachers.**

DEVELOPMENTALLY APPROPRIATE CHILD CARE AND EDUCATION

We view child care as a work force issue with two dimensions. The first is to provide working parents with a way to assure that their children are well cared for while they are at work and to enable low-income families to pursue training and employment. The second and even more important dimension has to do with the quality of child care as a critical building block of development and preparing the work force of the future. Child care does not precede and cannot be separated from child development and education. It is an integral part of the developmental base for all the children it serves.[1]

In short, we believe that the way we approach child care as a society can have both an immediate impact on work force effectiveness and a long-term impact on child development which, in turn, affect the work force of the future. We discuss these issues more fully in the context of the workplace in Chapter 6. The key point here is that the high level of attention currently devoted to the growing needs of many working parents for child care should not obscure the larger issue of how child care contributes to early-childhood development.

Quality early-childhood development programs for the disadvantaged are among the most vitally important investments this country could make. Successful early-childhood programs are a highly cost-effective way to compensate for the deficiencies that disadvantaged children suffer early in their lives by improving school readiness, reducing the need for remedial education, and enhancing later academic and social performance. In 1989, only 18 percent of 3- and 4-year-olds from poverty-level families were enrolled in Head Start; in 1986, 27 percent were enrolled in other types of preschool programs. In contrast, 42 percent of children in higher-income families attended some type of preschool in that year.[2]

In *Children in Need*, we describe standards for quality preschool programs. With the proliferation of programs at the state level, there are indications that quality is suffering. **We strongly urge that these standards for quality preschool programs be strenuously upheld for both newly created and existing programs.**

However, even the best early-childhood programs cannot address all the developmental deficiencies of disadvantaged children. Their effectiveness is limited if the children introduced to them have already suffered years of ill health or physical abuse that has left them permanently

---

HELPING PARENTS

The Maryland Committee for Children, with support from the State Department of Human Resources and the Lillie Straus and Aaron Straus Foundation, developed and conducted a pilot program in a Baltimore City Housing Authority and Day Care Center. The program was aimed specifically at reducing child abuse by young, low-income parents. (In 1987, 23 percent of babies born in Baltimore had teenage mothers, the highest proportion of any major city in the United States.) Gathering in the evenings for dinner and discussion, parents in a typical program shared experiences and were given guidance on how to provide for a child's basic needs, help build self-esteem, and control their own behavior in raising their children.

impaired. And even the most successful early-childhood programs will have little lasting impact if children go on to attend inferior schools.

The Senate Labor and Human Resources Committee has estimated the cost of high-quality part-day programs for disadvantaged 3- and 4-year-olds to be about $4,000 per enrolled child and the cost of full-day programs at over $6,000. There are about 1.7 million children eligible each year for Head Start, so enrolling all of them in such high-quality programs would cost about $6.6 billion. The $1.4 billion a year of federal money currently allocated to Head Start serves fewer than one in five children between the ages of 3 and 5 who live in poor families. **We urge full funding of Head Start for every eligible child between 3 and 5 who is not otherwise enrolled in kindergarten.**

PRIMARY AND SECONDARY EDUCATION

Traditionally, primary and secondary education have been viewed as encompassing the years of formal schooling, kindergarten through twelfth grade (K-12). Our public and private school systems are nearly all structured on that assumption. **However, we view education more broadly as a lifelong process, of which the traditional K-12 years are one important part.** Moreover, the time a child or adolescent spends in school during those years is only a part of the learning and development process. Equally important is the quality of engagement with family, peers, community, church, media, and other forces that affect young lives.

Since the early 1980s, an education reform movement directed principally at the K-12 years has swept the United States. Our 1985 policy statement *Investing in Our Children* played an active role in that movement. What has the movement achieved to date, and how should the energies for reform be focused?[3]

THE YSLETA PRESCHOOL PROGRAM

The Ysleta Pre-Kinder Center in El Paso, Texas, a model program, emphasizes five essential areas of development in which disadvantaged children need enhanced experience: (1) awareness of language as a means of communication; (2) the use of the five senses to observe the environment; (3) the development of motor skills, including physical coordination, balance, and fine motor skills; (4) the expression of creativity through art, music, and drama; and (5) social-emotional development for building confidence and self- esteem.

In its early years, the education reform movement was driven principally by state governments. The states, which provide just over half of education funding, recognized the importance of education to their economic performance. For the most part, these early reform efforts concentrated on top-down initiatives such as increased course requirements for high school students, higher standards of student achievement, competency testing, and merit pay for teachers.

There is little evidence to date to suggest that these reforms have had a measurable effect on overall student performance. Standardized test scores have not changed appreciably, and American students continue to compare unfavorably with their counterparts in other countries. Dropout rates of 25 and 30 percent since the 1970s remain stubbornly high.

There has been some success in efforts to improve the performance of black and other minority students. The National Assessment of Education Progress (NAEP) recently found that the gaps in average academic performance between black and Hispanic students and their white peers have been reduced, although blacks still perform at a level several years behind white students.

These early state reform efforts reflected a need for action, a response to the demand to "do something" that was simple, visible, and achievable and that held out hope for quick improvement. However, there is a growing recognition that there are few easy remedies; instead, there is an increasing sobriety regarding the depth and pervasiveness of the educational problem in the United States, especially in the context of world competitiveness. In some ways, the top-down initiatives may have increased divisiveness, and state leaders have begun to rethink education reform strategy for the long haul.

GOALS

There are fundamental skills and knowledge that all children need to have in order to function successfully in a more competitive world. But few public schools have determined precisely what their students should know and be able to do as they progress through their school careers. As a consequence, too many students are completing their educations without the competencies they will need in order to get good jobs or become responsible citizens.

The failure to identify desirable outcomes and develop performance-based goals or to measure how well skills and knowledge have been attained has proven to be a major impediment to successful education reform.

In the past year, some important steps have been taken on the national level and in some states to remedy this shortfall. The President and the nation's governors have provided critically needed national leadership by developing and mutually endorsing a broad-based set of six national goals for education. In brief, these goals state that by the year 2000,

1. All children in America will start school ready to learn.

2. The high school graduation rate will be at least 90 percent.

3. Students will leave the fourth, eighth, and twelfth grades having demonstrated competency over challenging subject matter including English, mathematics, science, history, and geography. In addition, every school in America will ensure that all students learn to use their minds well so that they may be prepared for responsible citizenship, further learning, and productive employment in our modern economy.

4. American students will be first in the world in mathematics and science achievement.

5. Every adult American will be literate and will possess the knowledge and skills necessary to compete in a global economy and exercise the rights and responsibilities of citizenship.

6. Every school in America will be free of drugs and violence and offer a disciplined environment conducive to learning.[4]

Significantly, these goals address not just intellectual achievement in primary and secondary school but also early-childhood development and continuing improvements in work force quality and lifelong learning.

The governors are continuing to work with the federal government to flesh out the goals and objectives, define more specific outcomes and indicators, develop strategies for implementation, and devise means of monitoring and assessing progress.

Nevertheless, we see these broad national goals as only a beginning. Public education is primarily a state and local responsibility, and there is considerable variation from community to community both in the quality of the schools and in the needs of students. **Specific goals for educational attainment and strategies for meeting those goals should be developed at the state level, in local school districts, and for each school. At the same time, the states should provide guidance and resources to help local districts and schools meet their goals, and local schools and school districts should be given wide latitude in deciding how to deploy available educational resources most effectively.**

We believe that every state and local community should take an inventory of its schools and the related community institutions that have an impact on the health, development, and education of its children. This effort should involve a representative cross section of the community, including business, parents, teachers, administrators, government officials, and civic leaders, to identify goals for students and the system, strategies for attaining those goals, and appropriate accountability measures to assess whether they are being reached within a reasonable time frame.

Major efforts in this direction are under way. For example, the Business Roundtable has established a ten-year project to work with governors and other leaders at the state level to identify, set, and implement education goals. And the NAEP will be developing new performance standards that will define for the first time what students in the fourth, eighth, and twelfth grades should know and be able to do.

Some states have already addressed the need for performance-based goals. For example:

- As the result of recommendations made in 1988 by a statewide citizens commission, Ohio is in the process of creating a results-driven education system. Performance goals are being set for preschool through graduate education, and an executive/legislative Commission on Education Improvement is being established to monitor results of reforms.

- Led by the California Business Roundtable, an educational reform bill was passed in California in 1983, which has halted some of the downward trends. Although test scores have shown some improvement in standards, and expectations are being raised, more has yet to be done in that state. A new comprehensive program of recommendations for restructuring education in California is under way, again with leadership being provided by the California Business Roundtable.

RESTRUCTURING SCHOOLS FOR PERFORMANCE

After a decade of education reform efforts, it is clear that a major restructuring of the public schools is still needed.

We believe that education restructuring should combine four objectives:

1. Clear and measurable performance outcomes compatible with established goals should be set.
2. Authority and decision making should be decentralized to teach-

ers, principals, and parents, with students taking greater responsibility for their own performance.

3. **Those responsible should be given the resources to do the job.**

4. **Incentives should be created for those responsible to perform, with effective accountability that rewards high performance and imposes appropriate sanctions on unsatisfactory performance.**

There are numerous forms that restructuring might take to achieve these objectives. Different approaches may be appropriate for different circumstances, a point that is especially important given the local nature of American public education and the diversity among communities.

There is no single public education system in the United States. Each of the fifty states has its own system, and the various state systems in turn are divided into more than 15,500 school districts. Only about 4 percent of the school districts enroll more than 10,000 students, but these account for 45 percent of all students.

The lack of a uniform national system of public education has certain clear disadvantages that can be seen in stark relief against the tightly organized and uniform national systems of Japan and most European countries. In those countries, national standards are set, a common curriculum is taught, and the performance of students and schools is carefully monitored through national standardized tests.

But although the decentralized American system may suffer in some ways, it also has certain advantages. It can, for example, facilitate experimentation with new approaches to education and be responsive to the highly diverse needs of students in this country.

The decentralized American education system lends itself to a stronger emphasis on the school as the basic management unit. It is at the school level that principals, teachers, and parents should share decision making and accountability for results. Many school districts, following such leaders as Miami-Dade County, Rochester, New Haven, and Pittsburgh, are moving toward *school-based management*, which, though still arguable, offers greater discretion for teachers and principals.

Dr. James P. Comer of Yale University, who has developed an innovative and successful approach to local school management, suggests that the most important element for a successful school is the development of trust among students, teachers, administrators, and parents. Similarly, in his study of high schools, John Chubb concluded that the best schools promote democratic methods of team building that create an atmosphere in which "the school seems like a big family." [5]

CED advocated such a bottom-up approach to education in our policy statement *Investing in Our Children*. However, we also envision an important role for states in defining goals, setting priorities, providing adequate resources and guidance, undertaking research and demonstration projects, and holding local districts accountable for results. Within that framework, local districts and schools should be permitted reasonable latitude to determine how those goals are to be met.

Vesting greater responsibility in the individual school is no guarantee of success. Even where such school-based management exists, some schools perform better than others, and some do not perform at satisfactory levels. There are numerous reasons for differences in performance among schools and school districts, including the availability of resources, the quality of teachers and administrators, the family and community environment in which students live, the motivation of students, and the methods of teaching.

Although all these factors are influential, the key to improved performance is whether those involved in a school have the *incentive* to provide their students with the best-possible education. We believe that most children have a natural desire to learn and that parents, teachers, and administrators all want students to learn. In other words, the underlying motivation is there; the challenge is to unleash it and channel it.

The problem is that numerous barriers to good results, such as excess paperwork, more teaching duties, and de facto school goals unrelated to education, have been erected over the years, suppressing the energy of educators or channeling it into wasteful or counterproductive activities. To tear down those barriers will require a sustained approach to rewarding high performance while penalizing and correcting unsatisfactory performance.

Some states have moved decisively in this direction in recent years. For example, Maryland recently adopted an accountability system that will evaluate the performance of students, schools, school systems, and the state as a whole, with corrective action to improve underperforming districts and schools.

Another approach to creating incentives for performance is the *public school choice* system, which permits students and parents to choose among competing schools and programs. This approach is based on a market model that assumes providers will respond to demand if the consumer has the option of giving his or her business to another provider. **We believe that public school choice has a potential to improve school performance if it is implemented wisely and as part of a broad strategy for restructuring the public schools. However, we also stress that choice alone is not a sufficient incentive for improved performance. Choice should be implemented only when it is one strategy in a broad restructuring initiative that emphasizes quality schools for all students.**[6]

Minnesota's program permits students to choose any public school in the state. Although only a small proportion of parents have decided to change their children's school, the availability of the option and the reality that some parents do choose to exercise it seem to have stimulated

---

MINNESOTA'S EDUCATIONAL PROGRAMS

The Minnesota choice plan is part of a broader educational program called "Access to Excellence" predicated on the idea that education should be equally accessible to people of all ages and backgrounds, and that the education system must fit the students instead of the students fitting the system. From newborns to senior citizens, Minnesota's aim is to blur the lines in the education system to promote lifelong learning. By remaining flexible, the plan creates new choices and new opportunities for students, parents, teachers and administrators. The educational programs in Minnesota include:

- Post-secondary Enrollment Options – High school juniors and seniors take college courses at the state's expense.

- K-12 Enrollment Options – Students, together with their parents, choose the public school they wish to attend.

- High School Graduation Incentive Program – Students at risk of dropping out of school, or who have already dropped out, are offered another high school or alternative programs to earn their diplomas.

- Financial Assistance for Higher Education – State aid supplements federal programs of assistance; state system of repayment based on income level of borrowers.

- Formation of Language Villages for Cultural Awareness – Students are immersed in a total cultural atmosphere over a continuous period of weeks.

- Community Service – The performance of regular service activity to the community stipulated in standard high school curriculum statewide.

- Early Childhood Family Education Program – School, parent, and child are brought together for health and developmental screening and educational schooling from birth to kindergarten.

- Educational Assistance for Young Parents – Payment of AFDC benefits are tied to school attendance; assists with day-care, child care and transportation needs for the school-aged student-parent.

- Educational Effectiveness Program – Leadership teams formed among teachers and principals to improve the learning environment at the individual school level.

educators throughout Minnesota's public school system to increase their attention to school performance. The Minnesota choice system is still too new for its performance to be evaluated fully. There are potential problems in the approach. For example, students who change schools bring with them only their state per pupil allocation, which amounts to about 70 percent of total per pupil cost. Schools may have little incentive to attract students if they must make up the remaining 30 percent of the cost. Nor is it possible for a successful school to attract additional students if its success requires remaining small or if its space is limited. Moreover, it is not clear how changes will affect the racial balance in schools.

Most of these potential problems are recognized by Minnesota choice advocates, who are considering corrective actions. For example, there is interest in permitting educators to open their own alternative schools within existing school districts so that parents and students would have a greater choice of public schools within their community.

CURRICULUM, INSTRUCTION, AND LEARNING

Conventional curriculum needs to be expanded to include a higher level of skills and learning ability. Advancing knowledge and rising world competitiveness require that a far larger proportion of our students become proficient in mathematics and science. And the internationalization of economic activity demands that young Americans learn more about other languages and other cultures.

Unfortunately, there is a growing mismatch between the increased flexibility and versatility required in the workplace and the habits that are implanted in students by the rigid organizational boundaries in our secondary schools. The basic method of teaching in schools has not changed markedly over the past century. Students go from one fifty-minute class to another "when the bell rings," and subjects are typically taught in nearly total isolation from each other. Indeed, the school environment resembles an old-line factory in most respects, even as business is introducing greater fluidity into the organization of work and recognizing the need for comprehensive and integrative, rather than segmented, approaches to problem solving.

A strong public commitment is also needed to improve the schools' performance in serving all youths by eliminating the neglect usually shown toward those who are lower achievers or slow in learning. New systems for teaching students who have fallen behind are springing up across the country and hold great promise for those youths interested enough to stay in school and learn the basic skills needed in the workplace. Escambia County, Florida, has instituted a program geared to the individual needs of such students, drawing on the experience of similar programs in Calvert County, Maryland, and Lafayette Parish, Louisiana (see box below).

Experimentation with such approaches is under way throughout the nation's public education systems. Many of these approaches to learning are also being developed in corporations, which are increasingly interested in the continual education and upgrading of the job skills of their employees. No single learning theory, curriculum, or set of teaching methods has

---

NEW APPROACHES TO LEARNING

The key to the new approach being tried in Florida, Maryland, and Louisiana is a computer program that individualizes instruction according to each student's present level of knowledge and ability, thereby changing the whole attitude toward learning. Students spend twenty minutes a day in a computer lab, reading problems and answering questions, each at his or her own level. The computer adjusts to the student's needs presenting feedback, tutorials, sequential practicing, prerequisites, and review as needed until the student demonstrates mastery of the subject.

Students who have known mostly failure in the past are now answering 70 to 80 percent of the questions correctly. Some have never passed a test before but now make the honor roll by getting more than 100 problems right in a week. Students who remain stuck at the same level for a week get extra one-on-one tutoring from their teachers.

The reported results so far would seem to be impressive. Twenty minutes daily at the terminal have produced academic gains of one to two years in just six months of instructional time. The system, designed by Computer Curriculum Corporation, also predicts how much "on-line" time it will take for a student to master a course. The students are given a new reason for staying in school and learning the basic subject matter they must know to succeed later at whatever they do; they can actually succeed at something and gain the self-confidence that comes from succeeding.

The teachers also gain satisfaction from seeing these particular students learn -- in many cases for the first time in their lives -- and show an interest in further learning. And the schools change their image of failing these students and benefit financially as well. The project is supported in part by the local Private Industry Council (PIC), which gives the schools $348 each time a young person who qualifies as disadvantaged under the Job Training Partnership Act (JTPA) gains one and a half years of grade level in math or reading. In its first year, only two of 375 JTPA-eligible youths dropped out of the program, and those who stayed earned $83,000 for their schools, giving them a further sense of accomplishment.

been proved to be superior to all others for every educational circumstance. Consequently, caution is in order in assessing the claims of new approaches. But unquestioning devotion to conventional approaches is also unwarranted, especially in light of continued significant deficiencies in educational performance.

We urge state and local school districts to undertake disciplined experimentation to discover the most effective approaches to teaching and learning in a variety of circumstances to improve student performance and to replicate successful methods. The key to achieving this is to structure the system of education in such a way that those responsible for educating children have the incentive, flexibility, and resources to constantly seek and apply the best approaches. **There is also a need for federal, state, and private-sector leadership to supply the resources and expertise required for effective research, development, experimentation, and diffusion of new approaches to learning.**

TEACHERS ARE CRITICAL

Over the next five years, about half of the public school teachers in the United States are expected to retire. Even though there has been an upturn in enrollment at teachers colleges after years of decline, there is still unlikely to be a sufficient number of qualified graduates to replace those departing. This presents a major challenge to schools, but it also holds out an unprecedented opportunity.

New, highly qualified teachers equipped to deal with contemporary needs in education should be trained and hired. It will be a major challenge to attract the numbers of qualified teachers that will be required. A National Board for Professional Teaching Standards, to be established by 1992, is intended to bring higher professionalism, accountability, and prestige to the profession. Greater consideration should be given to hiring qualified people who are not certified by conventional education criteria (as New Jersey has done).

These new, highly qualified teachers should also be more representative of the student population than teachers are now. In 1971, 88.3 percent of all public school teachers were white. By 1986, this figure had risen to 89.6 percent. Meanwhile, in the fall of 1984, only 71.2 percent of the students enrolled in public elementary and secondary schools were white.

To attract and retain qualified teachers in an economy short on knowledgeable workers will require offering salaries competitive with those paid in other sectors. This will be difficult for school systems facing tight fiscal pressure. Teachers' salaries declined in real terms during the 1970s, but increased 18 percent between 1980 and 1988. In 1987, teachers as a whole regained the purchasing power they had achieved in 1972. Average teacher salaries in 1987 ranged from $18,700 in South Dakota to $43,000 in Alaska (reflecting in large measure the difference in the cost of living from place to place).

However, the shortage of highly qualified teachers should be addressed not only by offering competitive salaries to attract the best people but also by compelling schools to rethink conventional approaches to teaching and learning. Greater emphasis should be placed on the use of technology and instructional methods that emphasize self-learning by the student. This will free the best teachers to manage the learning process in a more effective and efficient manner.

The nation's K-12 public schools collectively spend about $220 billion a year, but there is wide variation in the way these resources are allocated. Spending among the states ranges from $2,500 per pupil in Utah to $9,000 per pupil in Alaska (again partly attributable to differences in the cost of living). There is also a wide disparity of resources among local jurisdictions within the same state. Currently, some twenty states are under court order to redesign their school-financing systems to make them more equitable. And the proportion of total spending for administration can vary among school systems from 30 to 60 percent. **We urge every state to reassess the allocation of resources for public education to assure that money is spent on priority educational needs, especially teachers and learning in the classroom.**

THE SPECIAL NEEDS OF DISADVANTAGED CHILDREN

One of the biggest challenges is to meet the needs of the growing numbers of educationally disadvantaged children in the public schools. (CED discussed this issue in detail in *Children in Need*.) We define children as educationally disadvantaged if they cannot take advantage of available educational opportunities or if the educational resources available to them are inherently unequal. Conservative estimates suggest that as much as 30 percent of the school population is educationally disadvantaged.[7]

Although our society needs to do a better job of preventing failure by improving early-childhood practices, it will do little good to compensate for the deficiencies of disadvantaged children before they enter school if the schools they subsequently attend fail to help them overcome their remaining problems.

DIVERSE STUDENTS AND CULTURES

One of the principal challenges facing the nation's businesses and other social institutions is the racial, ethnic, and cultural diversity of the work force and of the society. The ability of social institutions to manage such diversity will depend in part on how well the public education systems teach students to deal with it in their formative years.

American schools have always been challenged to accommodate students from a wide variety of cultural, ethnic, racial, and class backgrounds. But in many ways, the challenge of diversity is greater today than it has ever been. Minority students are a large and growing proportion of public school enrollment. In fact, minorities comprise a majority of students in over half of the nation's major urban school systems. Family structure has changed dramatically as well, with far more students coming from homes with only one parent or with no parent serving as a full-time caregiver. The proportion of educationally disadvantaged children is large and growing.

The United States has always attracted waves of immigrants from diverse cultures throughout the world, and the public schools, from their beginning, have had to address this diversity. But here again, the challenge may be even greater today for several reasons. In the past, most immigrants came from Europe; and although their cultures and nationalities of origin varied widely, they nonetheless had in common the historical legacy of Western civilization and Judeo-Christian culture. Today, substantial numbers of immigrants arrive from every continent, resulting in a greater diversity of religions and cultures represented in schools.

POSTSECONDARY EDUCATION*

Higher education generally has been viewed as one of the strongest elements in the American system of education and work force preparation, and it will be all the more important in the future.

THE MULTIPLE ROLES OF HIGHER EDUCATION

Colleges and universities are responsible for educating a significant proportion of the American work force. Given the rapid pace of technological change, the increase in knowledge-based employment, and the globalization of the economy, higher education will continue to play a crucial role in developing individuals who can think independently and creatively and who can function effectively in a multicultural and intensely competitive world market.

Institutions of higher education have made major contributions to American competitive strength, especially to the scientific and technical base of knowledge that is critical to economic innovation. Research and

---

*See memoranda by DAVID PIERPONT GARDNER (page 162).

development are at the core of corporate efforts to improve the quality of products, strengthen production processes, and identify new market opportunities. Universities both conduct an important proportion of this research and discovery and train the future generations of scholars and scientists who will use and further develop this knowledge in academia and in business. Graduate-level and professional training will be critical to correcting shortages in such key areas as science and engineering, a challenge that will be all the greater because women, blacks, and Hispanics historically have not entered those fields.[8]

Colleges and universities are also responsible for preparing the teachers who will educate nearly all of America's future workers: early-childhood teachers, primary and secondary school teachers, university professors, proprietary and business instructors, and parents themselves.

Both in training teachers and in setting the standards for college entry, colleges and universities are influential in determining high school curricula and the quality of instruction. **Colleges and universities need to work in closer partnership with primary and secondary schools to assure that these critical linkages are reinforcing high standards in both basic and higher education.** Unless our primary and secondary schools improve significantly, the need to provide remedial education for new college students will further increase the demands on higher education.

Higher education will also play an expanded role in continuous work force training and lifelong education. Community colleges have already become a major component of work-related training in most communities. And both four-year colleges and graduate schools are increasingly important sources of adult instruction for workers seeking to upgrade their skills or train for new careers.*

Nearly 2 million students now attend private trade and technical schools, which train an estimated half of the skilled entry-level workers in the nation. Postsecondary vocational education also plays an important role in short-term career training, education for new careers, and lifelong learning, especially for workers in the small-business sector.

In general, the system of higher education has performed these multiple roles in a manner that has strengthened America's human resources. However, there are troubling signs of erosion in key aspects of this system that require vigilance or immediate corrective action. For example, the system is not serving all students satisfactorily, many poorer students are not attending college, and the connections between higher education and work force preparation are not being made effectively.

---

*See memoranda by ELMER B. STAATS (page 162).

ACCESS AND QUALITY

In recent years, higher education has come to be viewed less as a public responsibility and more as a private privilege to be paid for by families who can afford it or by students whose future earning power will permit them to borrow enough to finance their schooling. Symptoms of these trends include declining federal financial support for college students, the substitution of student loans for scholarships, and the sharply declining portion of total higher education expenditures coming from state funding and its replacement by rapidly rising levels of tuition.

Total nationwide enrollment in institutions of higher education grew from 12.1 million students in 1980 to 12.5 million in 1987.[9] This modest 3 percent growth did not begin to match the 42 percent surge in college enrollment that occurred in the 1970s, but it was higher than had been anticipated given the declining size of the traditional college student pool of 18- to 24-year-olds. The reasons for the higher-than-expected enrollments reflected both a slight rise in the proportion of 18- to 24-year-olds attending college (from 25.7 percent in 1970 to 27.8 percent in 1985)[10] and an increasing number of adults returning for upgrade training or education for new careers.

But while overall enrollment was rising, blacks and Hispanics were actually losing ground. The proportion of 18- to 24-year-olds attending college who are black peaked in 1976 at 22.6 percent and fell to 19.8 percent by 1985. The proportion of 18- to 24-year-olds going to college who are Hispanic had peaked a year earlier, in 1975, at 20.4 percent and by 1985 had dropped to 16.9 percent. During this same period, the proportion of 18- to 24-year-old college-bound whites increased from 26.9 percent to 28.7 percent.

The proportion of black and Hispanic high school graduates going to college also has declined. In 1976, the percentage of both black (33.5) and Hispanic (35.8) high school graduates headed for college actually surpassed that of whites (33.0). But by 1985, those percentages had declined among both blacks (to 26.1) and Hispanics (to 26.9) while increasing among whites (to 34.4).[11]

One reason for this shift may be that the cost of college has been soaring in recent years, outpacing increases in both personal income and student financial aid. The cumulative effect of these trends has been to make it more difficult for young people from low-income families, many of whom are black and Hispanic, to attend college. Between 1980 and 1989, the cost of higher education increased 55.8 percent in constant dollars at private universities and 30.2 percent at public universities.[12] During that same period, real personal disposable income increased only 16.2 percent on a per capita basis, and total available financial aid for college students increased only 10.5 percent in constant dollars. The consequence was that total aid as a proportion of total college expenditures in the United States fell from 27 percent in 1980-1981 to 20 percent in 1985-1986.

Today, private universities cumulatively are contributing more in grants for financial student aid than the federal government is. At some universities, one of every three dollars collected in tuition goes for student aid. Pressures to reduce tuitions, therefore, could also result in reduced student aid from that source for low- and middle-income students.

The combination of diminishing aid relative to college costs and the shift from grants to loans appears to be restricting the ability of lower-income students to attend college. In the face of rising costs, colleges and universities have tried to maintain quality by increasing tuition. This significantly restricts access for students from families of modest means. More subtly, it affects the career choices of those who borrow heavily to finance their education, by placing greater priority on immediate earning power than on the development of personal talents or long-term social contributions.

The increasing multicultural diversity and changing social values of college students are intensifying the challenges of creating an environment conducive to learning and to civil interaction among students and the university community. A Carnegie Commission report found that "the idyllic vision so routinely portrayed in college promotional materials often masks disturbing realities of student life," including alcohol abuse, student apathy, poor security, inadequate facilities, and racial tensions.[13] The success of our colleges and universities in addressing the issues of cultural diversity and changing social values will be a major determinant in the ability to deal with those same issues in the workplace and in the social life of the country.

INTEGRATING INVESTMENTS IN CHILDREN AND YOUTHS

If the various elements of child development and education are to be linked in a seamless web of services and support, integration of several types will need to occur.

First, the stages of development need to be linked to assure a smooth transition and continual flow of support as children grow from infancy into adulthood.

The institutions that serve children and young people at each stage are frequently isolated from one another. Early-childhood development used to be considered more or less the exclusive province of the family. Today, development in the earliest years of life involves a far more variable set of institutional responsibilities, including less exclusive involvement of families and greater involvement of public and private child-care, education, health, and social- service agencies. But the new pattern of institutional responsibilities is still in a state of flux.

For example, the distinctions among child care, preschool, and school tend to obscure the importance of assuring an appropriate combination of supervision, care, and education at each step as infants grow into toddlers and then enter programs of formal instruction. A 5-year-old child who moves from child care to kindergarten is the same child, but the two programs typically are operated by different institutions (community groups and the public schools, respectively), often with strikingly different organizational cultures. Without a smooth transition, when a child moves from one system to the other, the benefits derived from the earlier program can be quickly lost and the harm compounded.

The existence of formal systems of primary, secondary, and higher education provides a somewhat smoother transition in those years, although significant turbulence is still encountered by many students, especially those at risk, in the passage from primary school to middle school to high school to postsecondary institutions.

Second, related services need to be integrated to form a package of support systems for children and youths, especially for the educationally disadvantaged. Improvements in education need to be supported and supplemented by other community resources that reinforce and support the education process. The conventional distinctions among education, health, and social services need to be surmounted so that the needs of the whole person can be addressed more effectively.

Third, the various institutions and individuals involved in supporting and providing services to children and young people need to work in concert. These institutions include government agencies, business, labor, education, church, and civic groups, as well as parents and caregivers.

We recommend the following principles for integrating investment in children and young people:

1. Define specific desired outcomes.

Unless there is a clear and consistent focus on the desired outcome, efforts to coordinate, strengthen, or experiment with programs can quickly lead to administrative cul-de-sacs or wasted energy and resources.

Outcomes should be defined in the first instance for *individuals*, that is, children and youths, at different stages in their development and formal education. Related outcomes should also be defined for *families* and *communities*, as well as for other important targeted groups, such as *schools*, *school systems*, *social-service agencies*, and *businesses*.

2. **Create a comprehensive policy structure that focuses related clusters of services and institutions on those outcomes.**

Such a structure involves both top-down and bottom-up dimensions. The top-down dimension requires comprehensiveness encompassing the services and participants (including policy makers and leaders, service providers, and recipients) that bear on given outcomes and in providing a context for developing strategy. This involves identifying the appropriate clusters of services for each outcome, decentralizing authority and decision making to those in a position to act, providing adequate resources and proper incentives for performance, and assuring accountability for results.

The bottom-up dimension involves focusing on specific targets and structuring the system so that it produces results, with those closest to the need developing and applying solutions. The integration of programs and systems usually is most effective at the point of service delivery, whether it is the individual, the family, the community, or social institutions (such as social-service centers, nonprofit community development corporations, churches, schools, hospitals, and other local and regional organizations).

SUCCESS BY 6

United Way's Success by 6, in Minneapolis, recognizes that an early investment in a child's life is the best investment that can be made. Partners include business, labor, government, education, health, and the nonprofit sector.

The goals of Success by 6 are to promote understanding through child- focused public information, improve public policy by building a broad-based legislative agenda, and strengthen coordination of and access to programs that address the social, educational, health and emotional needs of children from the earliest stages of prenatal care to age 6 when they enter first grade. Other strategies include:

- A program designed to identify and encourage coordination of a community of service providers in the city and to make that community's members known and accessible to each other and to parents

- Programs to educate employers about the roles and responsibilities they can take on to improve the chances for young children's later success in school and life

- A legislative program to work toward improving state funding and policies for under-school-age children

For example, Minneapolis's Success by 6 focuses on *children prior to first grade,* integrating programs in all sectors that bear on assuring that children are prepared to enter public school (see page 53).

Baltimore's Lafayette Courts Family Development Center focuses on *families.* Case managers tailor a mix of related services to the needs of some 800 families (which include about 500 children below the age of 6), including health, developmental child care, adult education, employment and training, and family-support counseling.

Numerous efforts to integrate a range of developmentally oriented services focus on *schools.* School is the only institution that virtually every child between the ages of 5 and 17 attends. Through school-age children, it is also possible to reach parents and younger or older siblings. Such national programs as Cities in Schools have been integrating such services for many years. More recently, a number of the states have initiated school-based service-integration programs.

The Schools as Community Sites program in New York has targeted seven elementary schools in New York City and seven schools upstate to become models of education and social-service integration. Schools are to be used in the summer and after regular school hours to provide a range of health, recreational, social, and instructional support services. New Jersey's School-Based Youth Services is another example (see box below).

Business or the *workplace* can also be the focus for integrating services or delivery systems. For example, American Bankers Insurance Group Inc. in Dade County combines on-site day-care facilities with school for

---

NEW JERSEY'S SCHOOL-BASED YOUTH SERVICES

A statewide $6 million project in New Jersey, School-Based Youth Services, is one of the nation's most comprehensive efforts to coordinate services for high school students. Launched in January 1987, the program is administered by the state's Department of Human Services in collaboration with the Departments of Education, Labor and Health. It offers counseling, health, and Employment Services for 13- to 19-year-olds at twenty-nine sites at or near schools. For example, at the project's site at New Brunswick High School, the program is also linked with the Greater New Brunswick Day Care Council which helps pregnant teens find child care, and it coordinates health and dental screening, psychological counseling and medical treatment with the University of Medicine and Dentistry of New Jersey. It offers career counseling, and employment training in conjunction with a state-funded program and a local community college.

children in kindergarten through second grade and features continuing employee education, training, and wellness and fitness programs (see box below).

Other efforts focus on *communities*. The Kettering Foundation, community development corporations (and other community-based organizations), the National Civic League, and the Annie E. Casey Foundation all promote approaches that address the issue of child development and education as a community pursuit.

Some states and localities have established human investment councils (or work force investment or employment boards) to integrate services that affect the work force. Some of these are based on PIC and on state

---

INTEGRATING SERVICES AT THE WORKPLACE

The 1,200 employees working at the eighty-four acre campus-style headquarters in southern Dade County were the first in the nation to enjoy an on-site satellite public school for children in kindergarten through second grade. The school, which American Bankers Insurance Group, Inc. paid $350,000 to build, opened in 1988. It followed American Bankers' on-site day- care facilities, available to employees' children age 6 weeks through 4 years. Employees pay only $50 to $55 a week per child ($5 buys a week's worth of hot lunches for a child).

Employees with children in day care or the school are rarely late for work and are absent an average of 25 percent less than other employees.

The rest of American Bankers' benefits package is strong, too. Barry University holds on-site classes for employees, with American Bankers picking up tuition. And the American Bankers Management Institute awards employees $500 for each of the four levels of training courses completed. An employee who completes all four can earn up to $3,000.

The wellness program features two large fitness rooms with Nautilus and Universal equipment; a hardwood-floored, mirrored aerobics studio; showers; and lockers for a $5 monthly fee. Outdoors, employees are encouraged to use a vita pars course; canoes, paddleboats, and sailboats on Lake Landon; a basketball court; tennis courts; a baseball diamond; and a chipping green. Barbecue grills are available for weekend outings and company picnics.

For a nominal fee, a fleet of minibuses shuttles employees from other counties to work (workers commuting from Broward County pay $3 biweekly). Employees also can earn bonuses through internal contests and good suggestions (from $25 to $3,000).

SOURCE: Florida Trend (September 1989) pp. 51-52.

job-training coordinating councils that administer the JTPA. Others, such as the Michigan Human Investment Council, involve a more broadly conceived strategy and array of programs.

3. Establish a process that promotes productive interaction among key participants involved in achieving outcomes.

In addition to assuring that key participants, such as policy makers and other leaders, service providers, children, young people, and their families, are included in the policy framework, it is equally important that there be a process by which these participants can work harmoniously in pursuit of their commonly held objectives and reconcile their conflicting interests. Many communities and clusters of service providers are discovering that concerted efforts to collaborate, build consensus, negotiate common plans of actions, and mediate differences can facilitate the integration of services for children and youths.

One ambitious effort to achieve these ends is the New Futures program, sponsored by the Annie E. Casey Foundation. Still in its experimental phase, New Futures attempts to establish a process that involves all the key players in developing and carrying out a common strategy (see page 57). The vehicle is an oversight board in each community known as the Collaborative. It generally includes influential decision makers such as state officials, the superintendent of schools, heads of social-service agencies, clergy, and local business leaders, as well as individuals who represent potential service recipients, such as parents, community-based organizations, and students. The Collaborative plays a critical role in analyzing the local delivery of services and in advocating changes not only in its own organizations but also in the way the various organizations interact on youth issues.

4. Develop a cohesive strategy that is outcome-driven.

Effective strategies for the development and education of children and young people should stress several elements.

Resources wisely and effectively committed to preparing children and youths should be recognized as an *investment,* intelligent spending now to yield high returns and avoid costly remedial spending later.

Early intervention and prevention are essential to keep problems from developing in the first place.

Intervention for at-risk individuals should begin at the earliest-possible moment so that they receive the services appropriate to their needs in time to prevent more serious problems. For example, the earliest-possible contact a pregnant woman or disadvantaged child has with specific health or human services should link that woman or child with the entire network of allied support services. Many low-income mothers have their first contact with health care when they go to a hospital to deliver their babies, but by then it is too late to assure that they have had adequate prenatal care.

Pregnancy counseling for teenagers, pregnancy testing, food supplements, nutrition programs, and prenatal health should all be linked, and women who enter the system at any of these points should be immediately connected with the other, related programs.

Similarly, many disadvantaged children have their first contact with the support network when they enter kindergarten or first grade. Families in need, particularly those with young children who participate in a specific health or nutrition program, should be linked with the appropriate childhood-development programs, such as child care, parent counseling, and preschool. Attempts should be made to identify families or individuals in need early so that they can be connected with the services that will prevent their problems from becoming chronic. For example, schools that provide pregnancy-prevention counseling should also provide basic instruction on the importance and the availability of good health, nutrition, and professional care during pregnancy should that prove necessary.

NEW FUTURES

The New Futures initiative is a partnership between the Annie E. Casey Foundation and four cities (Dayton, Ohio; Little Rock, Arkansas; Pittsburgh, Pennsylvania; and Savannah, Georgia) and is aimed at developing comprehensive strategies for addressing the problems of at-risk youths. In March 1988, each community was awarded a grant of between $7.5 and $12.5 million to participate in the five-year initiative that has three stated goals: (1) to reduce the incidence of adolescent pregnancy and parenthood; (2) to increase school attendance, academic achievement, and graduation rates; and (3) to reduce youth unemployment and inactivity.

Each city has designed interventions that affect all facets of its local youth-serving systems. Examples of specific strategies include efforts to restructure middle schools in Dayton and Little Rock. In many of these middle schools, case managers work closely with teachers to create a more positive environment for students. Pittsburgh's strategy targets specific neighborhoods that are supporting New Futures Community Schools with community-based health centers. In Little Rock and Savannah, youth-wellness and pregnancy- prevention strategies focus on comprehensive health clinics that are in or near several high schools.

Strategies should also enable key participants, such as children, families, students, and teachers, who too often have been viewed as the passive recipients of services, policies, or instructions from others, rather than as active agents of development and improvement.

The *quality* of approach is crucial in order to assure that actions are addressing real problems and needs that will achieve results and are not just mindlessly carrying out generalized, cookie-cutter prescriptions that are ineffectual in specific circumstances.

5. Permit maximum flexibility for participants to tailor solutions to specific needs, adjust to change over time, and experiment with new approaches.

The circumstances of different populations and communities differ and therefore require different approaches. Moreover, conditions and needs change over time, and the strategies to deal with them must adapt accordingly. Experimentation and reasonable risk taking should also be encouraged so that new and more effective approaches can be found.

Although bottom-up approaches usually best serve these purposes, they also typically encounter formidable barriers, including legal and administrative boundaries of federal, state, and local programs and incompatible institutional cultures responsible for individual services. So part of the top-down dimension involves state and national leadership to assure that legislative, regulatory, and administrative practices are supportive – or at least not unduly restrictive – of local efforts. It is important, for example, that the funding streams for federal and state programs be flexible enough to permit creative efforts to integrate related programs. Some states, such as Massachusetts and South Carolina, have supplemented federal funds for programs such as Women, Infants, and Children (WIC). In Texas, the Board of Health opened the WIC program to competitive bidding and reduced the cost by $70 million, enough to serve another 95,000 clients.

One promising new direction is growing support from the National Governors' Association and other organizations for a comprehensive approach that links early-childhood education, services to young children and at-risk teens, programs to prevent middle and high school students from dropping out, and periodic skills assessment to identify at-risk students and provide them with appropriate remedial assistance. However, making such linkages work will require integration of programs that cut across agency lines and functional program divisions; programs at the federal, state, and local levels; and programs in both the public and the private sectors.

The lines of responsibility and action among government, business, and the nonprofit sector need to be more flexible if such approaches are to work.

6. Establish mechanisms of accountability that motivate and reward high performance while assuring that action is taken to correct unsatisfactory performance.

Just as effective accountability mechanisms are needed for K-12 education reform, they are also needed to promote high performance for the full range of activities that address the needs of children and young people. This means the clear identification of goals and outcomes, the establishment of measurable indicators, periodic monitoring and assessment, and follow-up action to reward high performance and correct unsatisfactory performance.

Chapter 4

The Education-Work Connection

One of the weak links in the American system of human capital investment is the connection between education and work. The sharp divide between institutions responsible for preparing people for employment and the workplace itself results from the long-standing practice of making a clear distinction between getting an education and getting a job. This distinction can no longer be maintained if Americans are to prepare properly for productive employment and find jobs that make the best use of their skills.

We believe that the two systems, education and work, need to be integrated in a manner that accommodates the close conceptual and practical relationships between them. Four principal ingredients will be required to achieve this integration.

- **Stronger business support for effective education.** Business needs to recognize that the quality of its future labor supply – the infants, children, and youths of today – depends on its support of institutions for childhood development and education.

- **Clearer identification of employability skills to guide educators.** There needs to be a precise and continual identification of the skills required for success in the workplace, and the translation of those skill needs into curriculum at appropriate stages of education.

- **A smoother transition for students from school to work at multiple points.** Students who leave school at any grade to enter the work force need to have both marketable skills and guidance in finding jobs and planning rewarding careers.

- **Improved entry-level training within business.** Given the widening gap between the skills needed in the workplace and those possessed by new entrants, business itself will have to play a stronger role in training new workers.

None of these measures suggests that education should be recast solely to serve the interest of employment. But they do imply fundamental institutional changes to assure that the education and guidance that students receive will equip them for success in the world of work.

BUSINESS SUPPORT FOR EDUCATION

Over the past decade, business leaders have become increasingly concerned that entry-level workers were not prepared to meet their need for skilled employees. The first place they looked for answers was the public school system. Not since the early decades of this century, when many vocational education programs were launched, has business shown such intense interest in the public schools. Many business efforts were directed at teaching high school students specific skills that would be immediately useful in the workplace, and providing them with information on the world of work through career-awareness days and work-experience programs.

But it soon became apparent that the problem was more profound. The public school system needed more than a quick fix; it required fundamental restructuring, both to correct chronic deficiencies and to meet the new demands of global competition. Business leaders who examined the education system closely discovered that the inadequate preparation of young people for productive employment resulted as much from the failures of families and communities as from the failure of the public schools. Thus, many have concluded that they have both a direct and an indirect interest as employers, corporate citizens, and individuals in assuring that children get a good start in life and develop their potential both as future employees and as citizens.

The seriousness and commitment of business to education reform is increasing. As we noted in Chapter 3, the Business Roundtable has undertaken an education initiative intended specifically to work side by side with governors and others in all fifty states and the District of Columbia to improve education.[1] The U.S. Chamber of Commerce has launched a major project to work with 3,000 local chambers on education reform. And the resolve of every major national business organization is reflected in the creation of the Business Coalition for Education Reform.[2]

The principal responsibility for education lies with parents, public school systems, government, and the community as a whole. However, business has an important role to play as a spark plug or catalyst to get meaningful reforms started, to press for implementation, and to assess results.

DIAGNOSIS, VISION, AND STRATEGY
Business should play a role in diagnosing problems, developing a vision of the new education system, and laying out a strategy for education reform.

The system of institutions that nurture and educate children in a community is far-reaching and complex. If a community's scarce resources of time, energy, attention, and money are not to be dissipated, it is essential that the most critical priorities be carefully defined. Business can help to shape a new vision of education as a lifelong learning process that is integral to social and economic life.

Moreover, in each community, strategies to achieve that vision need to be devised that are compatible with the local civic culture, as well as effective in addressing specific human-development problems. In our 1982 policy statement *Public-Private Partnership: An Opportunity for Urban Communities*, CED examined both the common elements and the differences in the civic relationships of different communities. Each has its own traditions, institutions, and styles, and these need to be taken into account if action is to be effective. Thus, even if the substantive priorities are clear, the strategies for addressing them must be tailored to the special civic character of the community. These lessons were reconfirmed in a CED-sponsored examination of successful business-school partnerships, *American Business and the Public School.*[3]

ADVOCACY
On the most fundamental level, **business should become a forceful advocate for education reform in support of children and youths.** With the political clout of their parents waning, the nation's young people need a powerful friend and supporter. In 1970, 45 percent at all households were occupied by families with children; by 1987, that proportion had dropped to 36 percent. Following World War II, the parents of the baby-boom generation represented a potent political force that spurred government to build and staff a flood of new schools. Today, families with children are a smaller political constituency and must fight to make the case for services for their children. There are also fewer nonworking parents with the time to devote to advocacy of schools and related institutions. The mothers who in years past would not miss a PTA meeting, school budget hearing, or board of education session and who would help

elect sympathetic candidates to the local school board, are now likely to be employed full-time and limited in both time and energy for such activities.

Moreover, an increasing proportion of the families that do have children are poor or come from minority groups that historically have not had the political influence to lobby effectively for good schools and supportive programs for their children. In addition, many of these parents are themselves at risk and not equipped to provide the kind of support and encouragement that middle-class children can count on to help them succeed in school. In many central cities, the public school enrollment is predominantly from such families, while the more affluent families have moved to the suburbs or sent their children to private schools.

The need for advocacy is not limited to disadvantaged children. Educational failures are widespread and affect all young people. More than ever, children and young people need a strong advocate, not to supplant the primary role of parents, but to supplement it. Business is one of the few groups with the combination of self-interest, resources, and political clout to take on that role.

COALITION BUILDING

Business should take the lead in building the coalitions required to achieve consensus on priorities for children and youths and take the sustained action required for tangible accomplishment.

Coalitions are required because so many organizations are involved in various aspects of developing human resources. Business is particularly well suited to deal with this complex array of needs and institutions because of both the substance and the geographic reach of its activities.

Coalitions are also necessary because it is rare in our pluralistic and multicultural society that a single group has the power to produce significant change. Leadership is required to build the constituency that can overcome resistance to such change. The most important determinant of whether children in a community succeed is how strongly that community wants them to succeed. The ability to build a coalition for their support is a test of that will.

DIRECT INVOLVEMENT IN SUBSTANTIVE EFFORTS

In addition to supporting improvement in the structure and operation of the system, **business should become directly involved in efforts that will substantively improve the preparation of children and youths for the adult world of work.**

Given the enormity of the problems facing public education, it is rare that individually sponsored business initiatives can produce significant change by themselves. Nonetheless, direct involvement in substantive efforts can be critical to the overall success of business actions in several ways. Through such involvement, businesses can gain firsthand knowledge of schools and human services programs and this knowledge is invaluable in helping them understand the nature of the problems to be resolved. Direct involvement can demonstrate commitment and help build credibility for business in its efforts to achieve more far-reaching change.

Direct involvement can be valuable either in experimenting with new approaches to learning (employing new technologies, learning theories, and organizational approaches) or demonstrating the value of established ones. For example, a group of Chicago-area business leaders has developed the privately funded Corporate-Community School for youths at risk, which is managed like a business (see page 65). In its first year, this new school served 150 residents of Lawndale, Illinois, most of them low-income blacks or Hispanics. They were chosen randomly from 2,000 neighborhood applicants to ensure a mix of students similar to that of other inner-city public schools. Eventually, the school will serve 300 students aged 2 to 13 in small classes organized by skill level rather than age to avoid the stigma of failure.

Other examples of direct business involvement in managing schools include the Committee to Support the Public Schools in Philadelphia, the Valued Youth Partnership in San Antonio, and the English High School in Boston sponsored by the John Hancock Partnership (see pages 68).

ASSESSING RESULTS

Business should work with the state and local school systems and the community to assure that a system of accountability is in place and used to measure, evaluate, and improve education and related programs.

Periodic reassessment of reform efforts is important for refining or redirecting strategy. The ten-year experience with education reform has made it clear that change will not be easy, that it is a long-term endeavor, and that it will require continual evaluation and adjustment of strategy.

EMPLOYABILITY SKILLS TO GUIDE EDUCATION

If educational institutions are to better prepare students for the new world of work, they need to understand that world and to teach in schools the kinds of skills and capabilities that their students will need if they are to be successful in it. To accomplish this, there must be a more precise identification of employability skills and a close and continuing relationship between employers and educators in order to define education goals that are compatible with imparting those skills.

In the past, schools and employers were left more or less to define their own goals for students and employees, respectively. This arrangement worked reasonably well as long as the American educational system produced enough qualified graduates who were ready to step into jobs and begin working, and the economy provided reasonably well-paid jobs for most work force entrants. But the situation has been changing.

CORPORATE-COMMUNITY SCHOOL

The idea for the Corporate-Community School of Chicago originated with Joseph Kellman, President of Globe Glass and Mirror Company, with the aim of "showing the public school system how a city school should be managed. This school will be a research and development laboratory for improving education." Set up like the old privately endowed New England academies (more than $2 million has been provided by sixteen corporations, including Sears and UAL), the Corporate-Community School has nonetheless been designed to operate under the same constraints as other city schools, with a similar annual expenditure of $4,100 per pupil.

The central concept behind the school is community partnership. This will be carried beyond the classroom by having teachers visit students' homes to encourage parental involvement, trying to give the children a sense that their authority figures (teachers and parents) agree on the importance of homework and other matters related to success in school. The school's principal believes it important to see home and school as part of the same support system. "It is crucial that children get a clear, unified message that school is important, and that people care about them."

The school will also serve as a social-services hub for the children and their families. A school office will work full-time matching needs with appropriate social service agencies, a process that usually takes a long time in the public schools, with matters referred to the principal, then a counselor, and so on. Operating hours will be from 7:00 A.M. to 7:00 P.M., so parents need not worry about leaving children unattended, and the school will run year-round.

Mr. Kellman now presides over the board of Corporate-Community Schools of America, Inc., which intends to open similar schools in inner-city neighborhoods in other parts of the nation. Like the Chicago model, they will rely on an authoritative school principal (much like a corporate chief executive officer) and be governed by boards made up of corporate sponsors, educators, and residents of the neighborhood.

Labor force and employment projections made by the Bureau of Labor Statistics indicate that occupations requiring the most education and highest levels of skills will enjoy the fastest growth in the decade

COMMITTEE TO SUPPORT PHILADELPHIA PUBLIC SCHOOLS

The Committee to Support Philadelphia Public Schools (CSPPS), the education committee of the Greater Philadelphia First Corporation, is an umbrella group whose mission is to stimulate, coordinate, and focus private-sector resources on the priority problems of education, with emphasis on the Philadelphia public schools. Its activities are coordinated by a number of task forces and subsidiary organizations, each led by a member of the Committee. These include:

Paths/Prism: An organization that draws on resources of colleges, cultural organizations, and corporations to provide intellectually rigorous professional and curriculum development for teachers. Its budget is $5.1 million.

Education for Employment/Cities in Schools: A broad and growing initiative whose goals are to reduce the dropout rate and increase the employment rate of high school students. Another goal is the overhaul of vocational education. Its budget is $1.2 million.

Financial Resources: A task force that reviews school district financial matters with the goal of identifying areas for management savings or needs for additional revenue.

Management Assistance: Various corporate involvements in improving school district management, with a major emphasis on human resource management.

Celebration of Excellence: An annual spring dinner honoring outstanding contributors to public education and a fall event providing cash awards to outstanding teachers.

CSPPS stresses long-term, major, systemwide improvements. It uses corporate dollars to leverage support from other sources, corporate leadership to get a range of institutions working together and following through, and corporate staff, as well as those of other organizations, as a source of expertise. CSPPS and its subsidiary activities have built a budget in excess of $6 million on a base of $280,000 in corporate investments. Foundation, government, and school district dollars make up the balance, with approximately $200,000 in additional corporate support to additional programs. The funds that CSPPS raises are used as seed money or as venture capital, with the School District picking up the costs of successful programs.

ahead. For example, health services and business services are projected to account for about 6 million new jobs, or 60 percent of all new jobs in the service sector, and both require many workers with specialized education or training. Indeed, more than half of all new jobs created in the next twenty years will require some education beyond high school.

The problem of growing skills shortages is much broader, though, as Hudson Institute researchers William Johnston and Arnold Packer have pointed out. They found that the average adult aged 21 to 25 is not even reading at the level required by the typical job in 1984. As an example, they cite telephone operators assigned to an information station. Not long ago, they only needed to know the alphabet; now, they have to know how to use computers and how to occasionally input fresh information. The chief executive officer of BellSouth Corporation reported that fewer than a third of the company's job candidates in 1987 met its basic skill requirements for sales, service, or technical jobs.

The Hudson Institute study constructed a scale of required occupational language skills, with a top level of six for people such as engineers and attorneys. Manual labor jobs are in the lowest category, requiring only "rudimentary" reading and communication. According to Johnston and Packer, the average job currently requires a language-skill level of 3.1, but the average level for the 26 million jobs expected to be created by the year 2000 will be 3.6. Meanwhile, the average language-skill level of new labor market entrants today is about 2.6, so they are well below the requirement for current jobs even as that requirement will be *rising* 20 percent for the new jobs of the next decade.

VALUED YOUTH PARTNERSHIP

The Valued Youth Partnership (VYP) in San Antonio, Texas, co-sponsored by the Intercultural Development Research Association and Coca-Cola, attempts to increase the sense of purpose and self-image of "valued" high-risk students by giving them the opportunity to tutor younger children. As the student-tutors care for and teach young children, they learn as well. Two years after implementation, the VYP program has achieved the following results: absenteeism declined; only 6 percent of the students in the program dropped out, compared with 37 percent in the county; tutors' grades, self-image, and behavior improved; and parents demonstrated enthusiasm and support. The success of VYP demonstrates the importance of building school, family, and community relationships to prevent high-risk students from leaving school.

Numerous studies have identified skills that appear to be needed in today's work force. Most include one or more of the categories used by the American Society for Training and Development:[4]

- Reading, writing, and computation

- Learning to learn

- Communication: listening and oral

- Creative thinking, problem solving

- Interpersonal, negotiation, teamwork skills

- Self-esteem and goal setting: motivation and personal and career development

- Organizational effectiveness and leadership

Few of these skills are part of the formal curriculum of schools. In *Investing in Our Children*, CED urged schools to adopt policies and practices that are specifically designed to encourage self-discipline, reliability, and other traits that are part of the "invisible curriculum" so important in imparting work force skills.

However, the definition of skill needs alone is not sufficient to assure that changes will be made in school curricula and teaching methods so that students will actually learn those skills. As Paul Barton has noted,

ENGLISH HIGH SCHOOL/JOHN HANCOCK PARTNERSHIP

The English High School/John Hancock Partnership in Boston provides an array of services for disadvantaged students, including tutoring and career counseling. The John Hancock HEART (Hancock Endowment for Academics, Recreation, and Teaching) program has established a $1 million endowment to support Boston's middle schools, particularly in the areas of athletics and support to at-risk youth. It provides grants to fund educational programs that lead to new ways of teaching basic skills, and provides essential recreational and leadership activities for young students across Boston. By combining scholastic and physical activities, HEART hopes to be a dropout-prevention tool as well as an overall school-improvement effort. Thus far, HEART has awarded more than $360,000 to schools throughout Boston to fund academic and intramural athletic programs.

"There is . . . a lot of room for different interpretation of the cognitive skills that high school graduates have acquired." Partly as consequence, "It should come as no surprise that disjunctures arise between learning in strictly classroom settings and actual problem solving" in the workplace.[5] The Young Adult Literacy Study conducted by the Educational Testing Service attempts to measure the information-processing skills that employers seem to want, rather than reading comprehension of school materials.

A major international survey of the changing workplace and skill needs by the Commission on the Skills of the American Work Force, established by the National Center on Education and the Economy, confirms the far-reaching changes that have occurred in the work force and stresses the urgency of restructuring education and training systems, especially for students who do not go to college.[6]

Better linkages need to be established between what is happening in business and what is occurring "upstream" in the systems that educate and prepare young people to participate in the work force.

Several national organizations, including American College Testing, the American Association of Community and Junior Colleges, and the American Council on Education, are working to establish a system to teach and assess employability skills as a means of improving the linkages between education and work. The Educational Testing Service is also extending its work in this area. Efforts have been made to establish institutional ties between employers and schools to help define and translate employability skills. For example, the Boeing Company has set up a network of education managers to work in partnership with school districts where the company has a large population of its own employees to ensure that graduates in those districts have skills that will meet the future needs of industry. The Secretary of Labor's Commission on Achievement of Necessary Skills, chaired by former Labor Secretary William Brock, is addressing this issue as well.

THE SCHOOL-TO-WORK TRANSITION

In the conventional relationship of school to work, secondary schools prepare young people to go either directly into the work force or on to postsecondary education. Those who go directly from high school into the work force theoretically are taught both basic and work-related skills that prepare them to step immediately into a job. The reality, however, is that American high school students, in contrast with their peers in most other advanced countries, frequently do not have good job skills and are left to fend for themselves in the job market. These inadequacies are reflected in the fact that between 1973 and 1986, the real earnings of American high school students who did not go to college dropped by 28 percent.[7]

The transition from school to work is further complicated today because there are more points of entry for a more diverse work force. In the past, most entrants were young people who had progressed through the formal school system and then entered the job market. But now a large and growing number of people already in the work force, returning to the work force, or entering it later in life require or seek additional education. They include workers who have been laid off, who have gone back to school to advance their education, who are seeking training in new vocations, or who are preparing to reenter the work force after a significant absence. Many of these new students are adults who have other responsibilities, including holding down a job and caring for a family.

There is also a wide variety of educational institutions and programs now included in entry-level training as well as retraining and continuing adult education: high schools, community colleges, four-year colleges and graduate schools, and proprietary schools. Each of these institutions needs to give closer attention to the way in which its students negotiate the critical transition from school to work.

TRANSITION FROM HIGH SCHOOL TO WORK

Most of our public schools fail to provide solid work force preparation for the majority of students who are not going on to college. Although these young people are heading directly for the work force, we generally do not offer them significant help in making the transition. According to the Commission on Work, Family and Citizenship, the average college student receives a combined public and private subsidy of $5,000 a year, whereas little is invested in the "forgotten half" of high school students who do not go to college.[8]

One program that has proven its ability to provide this kind of help is Jobs for America's Graduates (JAG), which now serves 12,000 students annually in more than 275 high schools in thirteen states. Each JAG program targets high school seniors who are identified as being at risk of dropping out or becoming unemployed after graduation. These are usually general education students with below-average grades and little or no work experience; more than half are minorities. Over a five-year evaluation period, JAG served more than 40,000 youths and "positively" placed 85 percent of them on the job, in the military, or in full-time postsecondary education or training. This is a significantly higher positive placement rate than that achieved by their counterparts who were not served by JAG.

JAG's national board is made up of governors, education officials, corporate chief executive officers, and labor leaders, representing the kind of high-level commitment needed to bring about substantial reforms. The program is financed with JTPA funds. **JAG should be replicated in every state to promote the school-to-work transition for those students who do not go to college.**

Vocational education is the neglected stepchild of the American public education system and is frequently dismissed by critics as irrelevant to the needs of students and employers alike. In *Investing in Our Children*, we set forth our concerns with the delivery of vocational education and the actions we felt were needed to assure that it prepared non-college-bound young people for the world of work. More specifically, we argued that:

- Much vocational curriculum did not relate to the work force and required substantial reform.

- Students graduating from vocational education programs needed to demonstrate a higher level of academic competence.

- Employees needed to become more actively involved in curriculum assessment and review and program evaluation.

- A vocational education degree needed to do more than signify a second-rate student.

Since then, vocational education policy makers at all levels of government have responded in many ways to the challenge. Indeed, some states, such as Oklahoma and Michigan, have developed very high-quality vocational education programs. Yet, much remains to be done if vocational education is to make the kind of contribution to employment that we believe it can and should.

Public schools can best prepare young people for employment by providing them with a well-rounded education that emphasizes learning skills, academic skills, interpersonal skills, and preparation for citizenship. Students should be well grounded in basic skills that will prepare them to learn job-specific skills throughout their careers. This does not mean that we endorse putting the majority of students on vocational tracks early in high school. But we should not dismiss the potential of *good* vocational education programs that teach both academic and more job-related skills. In designing such programs, we should be open to discovering the best attributes of systems from any country, being careful to adapt those attributes selectively to the American experience. As William Nothdurft observes in his study of successful European systems, "Schools and workplaces have been drawn together and programs have been crafted to guarantee that non-university-bound young people possess the knowledge and skills they need to secure rewarding work in growing, internationally competitive companies."[9]

Croom Vocational High School has been chosen as a national model by the National Center on Effective Secondary Schools (see box below). The school's principal thinks it is a model that can be replicated, but he is considered an entrepreneurial leader who ignores the conventional mind-set that leads to student failure instead of success.

CROOM VOCATIONAL HIGH SCHOOL

All new entrants at Croom Vocational High School in New Carrollton, Maryland, are certifiably at risk of failing to graduate from high school. A third of them have already dropped out at least once before, and most arrive with D or D-minus averages and very spotty attendance records. Within this context, Croom has a selective enrollment policy, admitting only half of the students it interviews. Success is considered the norm at Croom, whatever these youths' previous records of failure; the school thinks of itself as specializing in "new beginnings." The result is that 80 percent of the students complete the program, a third with full high school diplomas, and 95 percent of these land and hold jobs after leaving.

Half of each day is spent on shop work in vocational programs such as auto repair, building trades, maintenance and groundskeeping, child care, geriatric care, food services, and business occupations. Students maintain all the facilities at the school, prepare the cafeteria meals, run day-care centers for small children and the elderly, and operate an auto repair shop that is open to the public. The practical experience and the assumption of immediate responsibility connect them with the values of the adult world of work they are preparing to enter. This is one of the keys to Croom's success.

The other half of the day is spent on academic subjects (such as math, English, and reading) in small classes. The teachers are another secret of Croom's success. They are chosen more for their personal characteristics than for their credentials, and tend to have varied backgrounds and interests as well as experience in working with young people. They also have high expectations, which they communicate to their students, helping to produce better outcomes than the schools that expect such students to do poorly and let them know it.

The Philadelphia High School Academies also link the teaching of basic and vocational skills with work experience for students who could not qualify for vocational schools because of their low achievement levels. The academies are alternative schools within the city's high schools, and there are now ten of them. Two emphasize electronics, five specialize in

PHILADELPHIA HIGH SCHOOL ACADEMIES, INC.

The Philadelphia High School Academies program was initiated in 1969 by the Philadelphia Urban Coalition, in collaboration with the Philadelphia Board of Education, in order to provide disadvantaged, urban high school students with marketable job skills. The program has since evolved into a solid partnership between the school district and private industry and has expanded in several ways, including the development of curriculum designed to meet the needs of academically proficient and college-bound students. Beginning with the Academy of Applied Electrical Science, the program now includes the Philadelphia Business Academy, the Academy of Automotive and Mechanical Science, the Philadelphia Health Academy, the Environmental Technology Academy, the Horticulture Academy, and, as of September 1990, the Academy of Physical Education and Recreation, and the Hotel, Restaurant and Tourism Academy. As of September 1990, 16 neighborhood high schools will host academy programs.

More that 100 businesses support the academies, providing financial support, advice on curriculum and part-time and summer employment for job-ready students. Current enrollment is more than 1,750 students, most of whom score in the thirty-fifth to the sixty-fifth percentile on city-wide tests. The academies operate as mini schools-within-schools with their own administration, student selection process, roster, and curriculum. The program's success can be measured by a 90 percent attendance rate in schools which typically average below 70 percent, a dropout rate significantly lower than that of students district-wide, and a substantial after-graduation employment rate. Eighty-five percent of students who have successfully completed the program are employed or are in postsecondary educational programs, or both.

The Philadelphia Academies' approach is now being tried in California, where the Peninsula Academies are upgrading the basic skills of students at risk and preparing them for entry-level jobs in electronics and computer technology in order to meet the needs of employers in the Silicon Valley area. Local companies provide funds, instructors on loan, and summer and after-school jobs.

business, two focus on health services, and one focuses on automotive work (see page 73). New academies projects are starting up in Pittsburgh and Portland, Oregon. The potential for these schools-within-schools seems significant because their focus can be altered to meet the employment needs of the local labor market. **CED supports the establishment of more such alternative high schools in more cities.** By combining academic with vocational training, these schools can reach more students who are at risk of dropping out of school, and make them into entry-level workers instead.

Providing high school students with a solid skill base in specific vocations for which there are good jobs can be critical to assuring that young people get a good start in the workplace. Good vocational training, provided on a strong base of academic skills, trains a student not only for a specific vocation but also for the world of work more generally. Today, few workers need to fear getting pigeonholed into single vocations where they must spend their entire careers. There are abundant opportunities for retraining and learning new vocations later in life. The key is to get off to a good start with a strong base of academic, interpersonal, and work-related skills.

Even high school graduates who *do* possess marketable skills may confront difficulties in finding jobs that make the best use of their talents and offer promising careers because job-placement mechanisms have not kept pace with the increasing complexity of matching workers with jobs.

RECLAIMING THE DROPOUTS

The surest way to keep young people on the path to economic self-reliance and responsible citizenship is to keep them in school at least until they earn a high school diploma in a creditable program. But many have already left, and, despite all efforts, others will leave in the future. If it is difficult to prevent high-risk students from dropping out, it can be doubly difficult to reclaim them once they have taken this step. But there are programs that are doing just this, and they are a vital part of any comprehensive strategy for helping youths to enter the work force with useful skills.

The North Education Center in Columbus, Ohio, is an alternative school for potential and actual dropouts, whether they are youths or adults. School hours are from 7:30 A.M. to 9:00 P.M., which makes it easy for people to attend classes regardless of their schedules. Attending classes with adults provides the young people with some useful role models. North operates year-round on a five-term calendar. Courses last seven and a half weeks, and classes are an hour and a half or two hours, making them more intensive than the normal public school class. The center is a serious place, with no extracurricular activities.

More no-frills alternative schools like North that operate on a serious, businesslike basis should be established by school systems around the United States to reclaim some of the dropouts and get them

---

ALTERNATIVES FOR HIGH SCHOOL DROPOUTS

The 70001 Training and Employment Institute uses a competency-based curriculum to teach job-readiness skills that have been slighted by most training programs, such as resume writing, interviewing, showing up regularly and on time for work, dressing properly, cooperating with others, and maintaining a positive attitude.

After job-ready trainees are placed, 70001 staff members follow up with them and their employers for ninety days to see how they are doing and offer advice and encouragement as needed. This follow-up effort sets 70001 apart from traditional federal training programs that forget about their clients as soon as they are placed. One of the specific goals for each youth is to earn a raise or a promotion within the ninety days; this builds confidence and increases the sense of attachment to the workplace.

Trainees are also encouraged to upgrade themselves educationally, especially to work toward acquiring a high school equivalency certificate (GED); this is to prepare them to progress beyond the low-skill entry-level jobs in which they are placed. Remedial instruction geared to individual ability is given in reading, writing, and math. At some of its larger sites, the Comprehensive Competencies Program (CCP) developed by the U.S. Basic Skills Corporation is now available. CCP is a self-paced learning program using varied instructional methods, including computer-assisted learning, to maintain the students' interest. It maximizes the time spent on tasks and gives teachers more time to spend with students. Youths who have failed in school settings can achieve learning gains averaging 1.4 grades in math and 1 grade in reading after just twenty-eight hours of instructional time. CCP is now being used by schools and community-based organizations in 250 learning centers.

Another important feature of 70001 is its emphasis on building self-esteem. All associates (as the trainees are called) belong to a combination social and booster club that provides rewards and recognition for their accomplishments and offers experience in leadership and community service.

back to complete their education and enhance their chances of succeeding in the working world.

The 70001 Training and Employment Institute works with dropouts who are not going back to school, preparing them for the work force. Working through an extensive network of local programs in two dozen states, 70001 has placed nearly 25,000 trainees (75 percent of all enrollees) in unsubsidized entry-level jobs in the private sector (see page 75).

The institute and other programs that work with at-risk youths are often criticized for placing them in dead-end jobs, many of which are in fast-food eateries. We believe this criticism is misguided. These jobs are far better than inactivity; they are meant to be just first steps into the work force, and they connect these young people with at least the prospect for a better future. A study for the National Institute of Education found that work in a fast-food restaurant was one of the strongest determinants of employability for retail employers in general, whereas work experience in a "public" job had a significant negative effect on employability. Combined with continued training to provide new skills for upward movement, such entry-level jobs offer an important alternative for youths who do not finish high school. These entrants are expected to move ahead, but first they need to develop a work record and acquire some experience and at least rudimentary job skills.

A program that continues to serve an even riskier population of youths with some success is the Job Corps, the oldest federal training program. It removes these youths from their risky environments and brings them to residential centers where they are provided with a comprehensive range of services aimed at changing their attitudes and aspirations as well as giving them usable skills. This is an expensive program because of its residential setting and the clientele being served; the average corps member reads at a sixth-grade level, most are dropouts who have never held a full- time job, and many have had encounters with the criminal justice system.

Because the program is residential and rigorous, it has a high dropout rate of its own. Those who stick it out do better the longer they stay. Remedial instruction in reading and math, world-of-work training in job-search skills, and vocational skills training are all given, and completers show substantial success in getting and keeping jobs and earning higher wages.

The Job Corps has had as many critics as supporters. On balance, it has done a good job of helping those who would not otherwise find help because, for example, they would not have the initiative to enroll in a 70001 program. **The Job Corps deserves additional funding in order to reach more of these youths.**

ENTREPRENEURIAL EDUCATION

Improving basic academic skills in school is, of course, the biggest part of the answer to the difficult question of how to help at-risk youths succeed. But not all these people will respond to more traditional education and training efforts; some need to be reached in other ways, one of which is teaching them entrepreneurship to get them to buy into a work-based cultural value system.

At Jane Addams Vocational High School in the South Bronx, special-education teacher Steve Mariotti has put 300 students through a five-month "capitalist boot camp," the South Bronx Entrepreneurial Education Project. Companies formed by these students have registered sales of more than $100,000 in the past two years. According to Mr. Mariotti, the value of the program is measured less by business success than by the self-esteem that

---

JUVENILE RESOURCE CENTER

In 1981, the Juvenile Resource Center opened a take-out sandwich shop, the Lunchbox, in downtown Camden, New Jersey, using six workers from JTPA's Summer Youth Employment Program and $12,000 in borrowed money. The venture lost $25,000 in the first year, but in the process it trained and employed sixteen young offenders, paid them $21,000 in wages, generated $4,000 in income taxes and another $4,000 in sales taxes, and pumped needed money into the depressed local economy.

The originators of this concept of urban youth entrepreneurship have formed the Education, Training, and Enterprise Center (EDTEC) to help spread the concept to urban areas around the country. They have developed a curriculum called New Entrepreneurs, which seeks to teach urban youth how to identify business opportunities from housing projects to the suburbs. The program is now in both the junior and senior high schools in Camden; it is also active in Washington, D.C., Rochester, New York, Pittsburgh, Pennsylvania, Corpus Christi, Texas, and other cities.

For the past three summers, EDTEC has been teaching teenagers how to become contractors. It has now put 300 14- to 15-year-olds through a six-week program using outside instructors in accounting, law, and marketing to help them formulate their own business plans and learn the skills needed to carry them out. At the conclusion, there were business luncheons to which parents were invited. The program has consistently drawn praise from parents who want their children to learn about economics. Many parents have sat in on the course, and some have even formed partnerships with their own children.

entrepreneurship produces in these young people. Instruction in business math has also had the positive effect of raising their math-achievement levels dramatically while in the class. Mr. Mariotti sees some of these youths who are at risk themselves as natural risk-takers and therefore natural entrepreneurs. He now heads his own National Foundation for Teaching Entrepreneurship.

Similarly, the Juvenile Resource Center in Camden, New Jersey, viewed traditional training for entry-level jobs as only part of the answer and decided to start business ventures that would prepare youths for jobs by giving them marketable skills. Serving as both educator and employer allowed the center more flexibility in scheduling high school classes, work time, and time for teaching living skills (see page 77).

Aaron Bocage, cofounder of EDTEC, argues that programs such as JTPA should treat a portion of their funds as venture capital to use as loans and grants for youthful entrepreneurs in enterprise zones, and that other

---

AETNA LIFE & CASUALTY'S INSTITUTE FOR CORPORATE EDUCATION

The Aetna Institute was conceived in the 1970s by a chief executive officer who said that "the only resource that will distinguish us from other companies is our people." The company then started forecasting its future skill needs and thinking about how it would compete successfully to obtain these skills. The institute, established in 1981, is the answer to that question.

Its president describes it as Aetna Life & Casualty's vehicle for fulfilling top management's "commitment to education and employability." The Effective Business Skills School offers two basic skills programs: (1) to bring unskilled job applicants up to the level required to enter Aetna's work force; and (2) to raise low-skilled workers to higher levels that will qualify them for better jobs. Along with skills, trainees are taught values and ethics to help assure that they assimilate Aetna's corporate culture.

This continuum of training requires a major investment by Aetna, but it has greatly increased the labor pool the company can draw from in filling jobs and promoting people. Aetna's recruitment of new employees is aided further by its community education and training programs: the Saturday Academy for middle school students and Project Step-Up for high school students. These programs improve the basic skills of potential employees before they reach the job-application stage and make them likelier to choose Aetna as an employer.

national funding pipelines ostensibly supporting urban economic development should have similar requirements concerning youth enterprises. **CED agrees that federal policies concerning young people should allocate specific shares of funding for promotion of youth enterprises rather than continuing to put all the funds into traditional training and economic development programs.**

BUSINESS TRAINING FOR ENTRY-LEVEL WORKERS

Faced with worsening deficiencies in the basic skills of youths trying to enter the work force, some companies are tackling the task of correcting these deficiencies directly. They cannot wait for the public schools to be restructured, and they may not be able to move more of their activities offshore. Their alternative, short of automation or elimination of the jobs (including relocation abroad), is to provide the education and training themselves. The more directly companies get involved in basic skills training, the greater their likelihood of getting workers with the skills they need.

The costliest but most effective method is to do what the public schools have failed to do: train workers in the basic skills needed to do a job. This is not the specific task-related training that many companies have long done, building on basic skills that new workers brought with them. Training in many companies today includes teaching reading, simple math, personal grooming, and good work habits.

One of the most comprehensive corporate training facilities is Aetna Life & Casualty's Institute for Corporate Education. Established in 1981, it reaches about 20,000 people a year, either in person at its facility in Hartford, Connecticut, or through satellite television transmissions to other Aetna offices. The institute provides advanced education for existing employees and supplemental education for high school students, as well as basic skills training for new workers (see page 78).

Not every company is big enough to provide basic skills training itself, but employers can form consortiums to do this. For example, the Microelectronics Consortium Training Center in San Diego was formed in 1982 by a group of semiconductor manufacturers working with the local PIC to develop high-caliber candidates for entry-level jobs. Participating firms pooled equipment and expertise to get it started and are now enjoying its success (see page 80).

IBM sponsored its first Job Training Center in Los Angeles in 1968 together with the Urban League, and it has since sponsored seventy others nationwide. In 1985, IBM calculated that the program cost an average of about $3,100 per student and that graduates earned an average of about

$11,700 and paid $2,150 in taxes. By contrast, before entering, they had received an average of nearly $4,600 in public assistance. This investment in human capital benefits everyone—the individuals, their employers, and the society—in both tangible and intangible ways.

SAN DIEGO'S MICROELECTRONICS CONSORTIUM TRAINING CENTER

The center's primary purpose is to integrate disadvantaged people into the economic mainstream by giving them skills that will qualify them for entry-level career opportunities, rather than just jobs. Applicants need not be high school graduates. They must have low incomes and demonstrate some perceptual accuracy and manual dexterity, as well as some ability to read and follow written directions.

The three-week program teaches technical skills needed for such jobs as microelectronics assembler, and also covers job-seeking skills such as filling out applications, preparing résumés, and interviewing. The center advertises in newspapers and gets referrals from employers and alumni.

In the 1986-1987 period, twenty-eight companies of all sizes participated in the program. The center trained 163 people that year, and it has had a placement rate with local employers of better than 90 percent since it began.

IBM JOB TRAINING CENTERS

In conjunction with other companies, IBM helps start each center by providing equipment, curricula, management advice, and sometimes instructors. Community-based organizations, such as the Urban League or SER-Jobs for Progress, manage the centers, recruit and select students, place graduates, and raise operating funds.

The students, who pay no tuition, can receive transportation to the center if needed. The skills taught are geared to the needs of local labor markets, but all centers offer training in word processing and general office skills. Basic literacy and math skills are also taught, along with personal grooming and proper conduct. Students are expected to dress and act as if they were working in an actual office.

The 25,000 graduates have achieved a placement rate of more than 80 percent, and a 1986 follow-up study of 274 graduates found 93 percent still employed.

Chapter 5

Making the Current Work Force More Productive

The reality of increasing foreign competition has become painfully apparent to nearly all Americans. Our success in adapting to the demands of the international marketplace will hinge on our ability to become more productive. This will require making better investments in the development of our human resources and increasing the capacity of American workers to learn new skills and perform higher-value-added work.

The skills required for the jobs of the future will have to be learned and often relearned by both experienced workers and new entrants to the labor force. As the speed of change in the workplace accelerates, more training and retraining will be required. Workers increasingly will need more advanced skills just to qualify for the kinds of training that will be given. For some, this will require remedial instruction in basic academic skills that should have been learned in school. For example, workers in many manufacturing plants are now learning statistical process control, a system of quality control used widely in Japan but beyond the grasp of anyone who lacks a solid background in mathematics. Factory workers now have to "think sequentially" on the job, as one manager put it, something they did not have to do on the old assembly lines.

It may have been possible in the past to pay high wages to low-skilled workers, but it will be exceedingly difficult to do so in the unfolding service-oriented global economy that places a premium on knowledge and "brain" skills. Preparing the work force for these jobs will be critical to keeping productivity and real wage levels rising.

THE NEW AND THE OLD WORKER

Much has been said and written lately about the shift from a manufacturing to a service economy, from an economy based on the organization and manipulation of physical resources to one founded on collecting, processing, and distributing information. Knowledge and information have become the key raw materials of the contemporary economy, adding most of the value to what we make or deliver and making us more or less competitive. The people whose skills are required to create products and services of higher value today need to be educated, trained, motivated, and rewarded differently from their industrial predecessors who turned out large volumes of standardized physical items.

The old organization of work around a strict division of labor derived from the demands of machine-based production processes, with rank-and-file workers tightly controlled by supervisors. This model is rapidly giving way to new models based on different organizing principles. As the advance of automation and the almost limitless applications of microchip-based technologies transform the workplace, they are creating demands for workers who can operate more autonomously, making decisions and innovations on the job. In such a workplace, the ability to gain and apply new knowledge becomes crucial, and this creates a need for continuing education and training throughout the working life.

Technological change is not the only factor increasing the skills required to perform many jobs; the move toward greater decentralization of decision making is creating similar demands. In these less hierarchical organizational structures, workers gain more authority to make decisions affecting the company's products and customers.

While employers are leveling organizational structures by removing layers of management, they are also "downsizing" their permanent work forces, using part-time and temporary employees as well as outside contractors. This is making more workers responsible for their own career development because the historical bonds tying them to a particular employer are loosened.

WORKPLACE TRAINING AND LEARNING

Employers spend at least $30 billion annually on formal training of their workers and anywhere from $90 billion to $180 billion for informal training, which might include watching other workers do the job or receiving instruction outside formal program settings. These larger estimates for informal training include the *opportunity costs* of salaries and wages paid to workers while they are being trained. The average U.S. company currently spends about 1 percent of payroll on formal training, and a few employers are devoting as much as 3 or 4 percent to this purpose.[1]

By any estimate, then, workplace training and learning in American industry constitute a huge enterprise. Yet, most of the people involved in it do not perceive themselves as part of an overall system. Only recently has such training been recognized as a professional activity and an institutional function in the business world. This is a development that bodes well for a future in which skilled workers will change the nature of their work several times during their careers.

A few large companies have not only recognized the importance of education and training but have also translated this recognition into major commitments of time and money.

For example, Aetna Life & Casualty's Institute for Corporate Education (discussed in Chapter 4) provides both basic skills training for new workers and advanced training for existing employees.

When Nissan built an automobile plant in Smyrna, Tennessee, it spent $63 million (including $9 million from the Tennessee state government) to train a new work force of 2,500 people, an average of $25,000 per employee. About a third of those employees, including managers, engineers, factory workers, and maintenance workers, were sent to work as companions in Nissan plants in Japan and then returned to Tennessee to train other American employees. Nissan executives believe the quality of production in the Smyrna plant is as good as or better than that in any of their plants in Japan.

IBM assigns all direct education and training expenses to a separate cost center. With operating revenues of about $50 billion in 1988, the company spent almost $1 billion for the salaries of its 7,000 in-house instructors and the upkeep of the physical plant associated with these activities, an impressive campus near the corporate headquarters in Armonk, New York. When the imputed value of the salaries of all its employees who underwent any training is included (20,000 employees, or 5 percent of its work force, are involved in training on any given day), the total sum is $2 billion, or 4 percent of the company's revenues.[2] IBM spends this much on education and training because it recognizes the payoff in improved competitiveness and profitability.

In 1986, IBM began a fundamental restructuring of its employee education system aimed at improving quality while containing costs (see page 84). So far the company is saving about $175 million a year as a result of using this new method for delivering education, and expects to save $250 million a year when it is fully installed. The education system is now built into IBM's business operating plan as well and therefore has become a part of the larger management system.

The importance of education is obvious for high-technology firms such as IBM that are clearly in the knowledge business and must keep improving and upgrading that knowledge. But the importance is not yet so obvious to most companies, which often question making such large investments in training when the returns will be realized by the trainees or by other employers that do not make similar investments but simply hire away well-trained employees of those firms that do. Although education and training benefit the economy as a whole and thus employers in general,

---

EDUCATION AT IBM

IBM has been redesigning its approach to the job-related education of its employees. It begins by identifying the specific jobs that need to be performed (eighty-five separate jobs have been designated) and the specific knowledge and skills that are required to perform each job at entry, journeyman, and expert levels. Courses are designed to teach that knowledge and those skills, and if any students do not master the material, it is assumed that the deficiency lies in the teaching system, not in the student.

The IBM courses employ a wide range of methods and technologies geared toward highly interactive learning by the individual at his or her own pace. Students work with computers and various video and audio technology or in groups using electronic classroom technology to engage them and provide the teacher with constant feedback on whether they are learning.

The IBM system uses a four-level series of performance measurements: (1) student satisfaction; (2) tested mastery of the material; (3) application of the acquired knowledge and skills to the specific job the employee performs; and (4) the impact of improved performance in those jobs on overall business results. The company expected to take five years to implement all these measurements of performance. As of 1989, corporate educators had developed successful measurement systems for the first two levels, were in the process of developing measures for the third level, and had yet to systematically address the fourth (although the consensus among management appeared to be that the new educational system *had* made a contribution to business results).

Another key to the system is enhanced status for the teachers within IBM's corporate ranks. New job levels and career paths were established, and pay levels were raised to comparability with those of engineers and salespeople. The company wants to have outstanding people doing the teaching because it sees them as the ones who give employees the wherewithal to be a competitive work force.

much of this gain is not realized directly by the employer doing the training.

Nonetheless, the incentives for all firms to invest in education and training will continue to increase, even in industries not typically viewed as high tech. An interesting example is provided by Burger King Corporation, which operates in an industry noted for low wages, high turnover, and little formal training for most workers. In an effort to reduce the cost of high turnover, Burger King has agreed to set aside as much as $2,000 per employee in a special education and training fund for those who attain a specified length of service. In its restaurants where this has been put into effect, turnover has been more than halved, and the program has more than paid for itself.[3] This initiative has been dubbed a "private-sector GI Bill."

Learning on the job, just like higher levels of education or investments in new technology, produces positive returns in the form of enhanced productivity. But with the returns from such learning spread across society and the costs of developing applied training programs high, American business is underinvesting in employer-based learning just when demographic and economic trends are making the ability to learn in the workplace more crucial to its competitive position. Companies such as IBM and Aetna tend to be exceptions to the rule of inadequate commitment by employers to continuous learning. Indeed, this is a weak link in the overall system for developing human resources. As a nation, we invest heavily in formal education to prepare people for adult working life, but we fail to follow up sufficiently to develop and make optimum use of this human capital in the workplace.

The high costs of formal training programs tend to restrict them to elite professional and technical workers, where returns are predictably high. But those who used to be considered production workers are becoming more important now as the skill content of *their* jobs rises, and training is gradually being extended to more of them. Nevertheless, we are falling far short of capturing all the potential gains in productivity and competitiveness that might be achieved by increasing investments in educating and training these workers.

The best examples of the ways new technologies are increasing the range of skills required to perform most jobs are found on the shop floor. Where the skilled machinist used to head a team that included a materials handler, an operator/assembler, and a maintenance person, these jobs have all been transmuted into that of the technician who oversees an automated manufacturing process. This technician must have a wider variety of basic skills than any of the workers who performed the other jobs, and there is a strong need for higher levels of reading, writing, and computational skill to understand technical manuals and exercise control over complex, numerically based machinery. Because of the greater autonomy, the technician also must have better-developed personal management skills and a new set of adaptive skills: "learning to learn," creative thinking, and problem solving.[4]

Similarly, new information technologies have created greater capacities to customize products in both manufacturing and services. This also requires adaptive learning and problem-solving skills on the part of employees who are actually making the goods and delivering the services and stronger communication skills for dealing with fellow workers, suppliers, and customers.

TRAINING AND SMALL BUSINESSES

A study by the Small Business Administration found that only about 9 percent of workers in firms with 50 to 99 employees received any formal training in their first three months on the job, compared with 29 percent of workers in firms with 500 to 2,000 employees. Overall, only 20 percent of employees in these small businesses get *any* formal training at all, and only a third ever get any training on the job, yet, two-thirds of all workers hold their first job in such companies.

There are various options for those employed by smaller companies to receive training. For example, some smaller companies can form consortiums to provide training that none of them could afford individually. A good example of this is the Microelectronics Consortium Training Center described in Chapter 4. But this example was taken from a high-tech manufacturing industry that has relatively high-value-added jobs for which such investments have obvious returns. Most small employers are low-tech service providers and must rely on the traditional training system supported by the larger public. Large firms can also help small firms with training and should be especially motivated to do so if the small firms are suppliers or otherwise involved in the enterprise of the large firm (see page 87).

EMPLOYER STRATEGIES AND PUBLIC POLICY INCENTIVES

Employers' current investment in formal learning for their workers is less than 2 percent of their payroll and covers only a little more than 10 percent of all employees. Many employers may want to consider spending more money to provide training to more of their employees. But by itself, spending more is not the answer. Companies also need to follow examples such as that of IBM and make development of human resources an integral part of their organizational structures and corporate cultures. This will require them to link training and learning to manage their human resources (hiring, evaluating, and rewarding employees). They must then link human resource management to strategic planning, as they do with other corporate disciplines such as marketing and finance. **Upgrading employees' skills continually to meet the evolving requirements of jobs will be a key to innovation and competitiveness and hence to future business performance.**

Many employers have tried to train their workers for other opportunities within the company. But as new technologies reduce the job-specific nature of skills and increase more general skill requirements, employers will gain greater benefits from generic skills training. This could even mean shifting the locus of some in-house training to outside institutions such as community colleges and private proprietary schools. For example, Pacific Telesis Group created its own Telesis Management Institute in 1985 to promote three objectives for its employees: engaging their minds, empowering their futures, and extending their educations. To do this, the Institute has a self-directed education program in which more than 500 employees were enrolled on-site in 1987 (see page 88).

LARGE HELPING SMALL

Large firms can help smaller firms in training their employees. The Large Helping Small Program was created in response to the challenge of small businesses training in Connecticut. Following up on a recommendation made by Jobs for the Future that large companies should share their training resources with small companies, Southern New England Telephone and Mohegan Community College have implemented the first in a series of training seminars. Through this partnership, SNET made available to small businesses a top-quality training program for first line supervisors at one-quarter the cost they would have paid on the market. Small business participants rated the course one of the best they had ever taken; the program will be expanded. Given the many obstacles preventing employees of small businesses from getting the training they need and the interdependent relationship between large and small companies, a partnership such as this one is a winning solution for all those involved.

SOURCE: Jobs for the Future

Public policy could give a strong new impetus to workplace learning. The simplest, most direct way to do this would be through the tax system, which does not currently favor employer investments in education and training in the way it has encouraged investments in capital equipment through accelerated depreciation allowances and investment tax credits.

A tax policy that favors investment in new capital goods and technologies slights the importance of human knowledge and skills to the success of the enterprise. Tax benefits to promote greater development of human resources would have the effect of spreading the employers' costs of investing in human capital across the society, which ultimately derives economic benefits regardless of where the workers may go with their new skills. A tax credit for training would raise its status within the business sector and, by formalizing activities that now occur informally, would improve the quality of the training that takes place and encourage a more coherent and universal approach to bringing lifetime learning to the workplace.

Tax benefits can be criticized on the ground that they unnecessarily subsidize activity that would have taken place anyway. But in the case of investments in human capital, as in the case of investment in research and

---

TELESIS MANAGEMENT INSTITUTE

The institute goes well beyond other companies' tuition-reimbursement policies by facilitating self-directed education on company premises in collaboration with California colleges. When fifteen or more employees form a "cohort" interested in a particular subject, the institute contacts the appropriate school to set up a course integrated into a degree program. The school provides instruction, counseling, and testing; the institute provides space, covers tuition, and helps employees match programs with their career goals. Students can obtain degrees on an accelerated basis without having to leave company premises.

Pacific Telesis sees its emphasis on continuing education as important for two reasons: (1) providing upward mobility for minorities and women, who make up an increasing share of its work force, and (2) helping the company to keep up with technological change in its industry. A company official stated that without continuing education, it would not be able to compete with the Japanese. Says one Pacific Telesis executive, "Employees and management both know education is important. They can see the handwriting on the terminal screen!"

development and in plant and equipment, a credit that covers only a portion of the cost would still require a major commitment on the part of employers. **To reach the maximum number of employers, the credit should be made usable even by companies that have no taxable earnings. And to the extent this can be determined, it should apply only to new training beyond what an employer already provides.**

There is evidence that corporate spending under the earlier tax credit for R&D increased by the same percentage as the amount of the credit.[5] If a tax credit for training had a similar effect, and if it covered 20 percent of the costs of new training programs, employer spending on training could be expected to increase by $6 billion from its present level of $30 billion at a cost to the federal treasury of about $600 million in forgone revenues. Again, if the evidence from R&D spending is an accurate guide, the benefits to trainees and to society emanating from that spending would be several times the benefits to employers themselves. Of course, any added cost to the federal treasury is a hard sell in the present fiscal climate. But some of this lost revenue would probably come back in the form of additional corporate taxes that would result from increased corporate earnings. Moreover, trainees' wages should be higher as a result, thus increasing personal income tax revenues.

STATE INITIATIVES

The states are also tackling the task of helping workers respond to the changing demands of the workplace. Virtually every state has adopted some kind of customized training strategy, often in conjunction with economic development efforts to attract new employers to the state. In our 1986 policy statement *Leadership for Dynamic State Economies*, CED encouraged states to give greater attention to developing jobs and retaining workers within their borders, which many are now doing. This expanding perspective is shifting the states' focus from public job-preparation programs to the employers' internal training systems.

While the size of employer training efforts dwarfs state investments in training, some states have pursued ways of using their limited funds to demonstrate the value of investing in human capital and to leverage private-sector spending. Most states do not relate eligibility to income, thereby allowing all kinds of workers to make use of these programs.

Several states focus their programs on potentially dislocated workers. California's Employment Training Panel and the Delaware Blue Collar Jobs Act were both established for this purpose. These two programs are also noteworthy for using the state unemployment insurance system to finance their services.

Several states have established quasi-governmental organizations to administer their job-specific training programs. They have not only removed control from traditional executive agencies, but their organizations also directly involve business in state-funded efforts to improve workers' skills. These skills corporations seek to develop partnerships between businesses and educational institutions that will help build the capacity of those institutions to provide some of this training. For example, they may offer funding to develop a curriculum that will enable the school to help area industries.

Kentucky's Bluegrass State Skills Corporation helped the industrial technology departments of two universities to improve their curricula so that they, in turn, could help companies prepare their workers to deal with the technological demands of robotics and computer-aided design and manufacturing (CAD/CAM), and with the new work processes involved in flexible manufacturing. This helps keep the institutions in a position to prepare students for the technological requirements of new jobs, as well as keeping current workers' skills up to date.[6]

TRAINING INCENTIVES FOR WORKERS

Widespread recognition of the need for continuing retraining to keep workers abreast of the increasing technical demands of the workplace has enlivened the discussion of how individuals can be encouraged to invest in training themselves. Among the ideas that have been advanced are the individual training account (ITA), training vouchers, and the training bank. With the ITA, employers and workers would both contribute to a fund that would then be available for training in the event of dislocation.

The idea of a voucher for training has parallels in other areas of social and economic policy, from elementary education to Medicare. It could be funded with contributions from employers and workers into special voluntary funds, such as the one established under the United Autoworkers' contract with the Big Three automakers that has been used to help displaced autoworkers gain skills to make them employable in other occupations. However, like ITAs, these vouchers benefit only the unemployed; workers who remain employed would receive only the very limited tax incentive available under the current tax code. (Currently, deductions are confined to expenses incurred for job-related training, which covers only skills used in an existing trade but not those that would qualify the worker for a new one). This tax policy deters individuals from investing in their own human capital, and it should be changed. **CED believes the deduc-**

tion should be broadened to cover acquisition of skills needed in a new occupation as well as a current one.

An idea modeled on some European programs would cover workers whatever their employment status. The *training bank* concept would create a kind of human resource investment account funded by a payroll tax on both employers and workers. One version would limit its use to workers with at least five years of experience and would pay for up to two years of training beyond high school at a variety of institutions anytime during the working life. Another would create a national trust fund financed by a one-cent-an-hour payroll tax on both employers and employees, which would yield an estimated $3 to $4 billion annually.

Some states have already experimented with training trust funds of this kind. Delaware was the first, requiring employers to pay an additional 0.1 percent on top of the existing unemployment tax rates; this assessment provides at least $1.6 million annually to fund new training under the state's Blue Collar Jobs Act.

California now raises $55 million annually from a similar tax to run its Employment Training Panel. The panel, which is made up of business, labor, and government members, contracts with schools or employers to establish training programs. Schools must show that they have arranged with particular employers to provide specified kinds of training to workers who are receiving unemployment benefits, who have exhausted their benefits within the past year, or who are likely to become unemployed unless they are retrained. This program is broader in coverage than the ITA and voucher plans proposed at the federal level because it tries to prevent obsolescence rather than just deal with its aftermath. Trainees must remain in training-related jobs for at least ninety days at a minimum wage of $5 an hour in order for funds to be released. Grants are also made to firms to promote development of models for in-house training. **CED urges other states to establish programs to encourage business training initiatives.**

CHANGING LABOR MARKET INSTITUTIONS

Within the labor market, there are important institutional barriers to the kinds of changes needed to develop a more competitive work force for the future. Two of these barriers are the present unemployment insurance system and the U.S. Employment Service as currently operated. Our recommendations for changing these two labor market institutions overturn conventional thinking about them, something that we believe is long overdue.

UNEMPLOYMENT INSURANCE AND RETRAINING: DISLOCATED WORKERS

The idea of using the unemployment insurance (UI) system to fund retraining for workers who are displaced by economic change has been discussed for years, and opportunities already exist to do this. For example, a 1970 change in the law allowed workers to enroll in training without losing their benefits if they continue actively to seek work. But this opportunity was not energetically pursued because facilitating training was not seen as part of the mission of the UI system. Although a few states, including Hawaii and West Virginia, were already trying to make training opportunities available, the 1970 law does little more than support an appeal by any claimant who is denied benefits while enrolled in training; states need make no active efforts to promote training in order to satisfy its terms.

Much could be done to implement the 1970 amendments more proactively. For example, it would be useful to involve the state vocational education agencies that provide retraining in a working partnership with the Employment Service and state labor departments, or to develop active outreach to UI claimants and build collaborative efforts to match displaced workers with job-training opportunities in the community. If the Employment Service is actively involved in the local JTPA Title III program for serving displaced workers, for example, it can identify UI claimants who are the best candidates for training.

Beyond using UI trust funds directly, Paul Barton of the Educational Testing Service suggests two options for doing more to provide training. The first is to emulate the Delaware and California examples and use the UI payroll tax system to collect an additional earmarked tax. The second, and more ambitious, would be to extend the social insurance concept expressed in UI to provide what he calls "retraining risk protection," to be paid for by employers and workers; it would cover displaced workers who lack prospects for reemployment without retraining or further education and who had worked long enough to show a visible attachment to the work force.[7]

In the new demographic world, the United States will need experienced people in the work force, and we should invest in retooling their skills. **CED urges adoption of a second-tier individual account under the unemployment insurance system, financed with a portion of the current employer tax, to encourage laid-off workers to seek training for other jobs that are in demand.** This idea was originally proposed by Kenneth McLennan of the Manufacturers' Alliance for Productivity and Innovation.

Title III of the JTPA also encourages a link between receipt of UI benefits and promotion of retraining. States may use their UI payments to satisfy up to half of the 50 percent matching-funds requirement under JTPA. This illustrates how better coordination among the various parts of the publicly supported training system could do much to advance the cause of retraining displaced workers, even in the absence of any structural changes in just the UI system.

Companies can provide training to help their own displaced workers develop the skills to find jobs with other employers. They can do this either through in-house programs or by subsidizing external education and training with allowances or tuition-refund payments. The Ford Motor Company, for example, offers career counseling and job development, including tuition assistance, as part of a comprehensive program for its workers (see page 94).

THE EMPLOYMENT SERVICE AND WORKER MOBILITY

The federal and state Employment Service is responsible for matching job seekers with vacancies, through testing, assessment, and referral. Although a few states have succeeded in making it a useful source of information on job markets and individual job seekers' skills, there is continued dissatisfaction with the employment service in many states.

Given the potential importance of its role, the Employment Service should be made much more effective. As the Commission on Work Force Quality and Labor Market Efficiency has noted, the most promising way to do this is to develop a system of accountability similar to that used for the JTPA. An earlier attempt at establishing accountability in the service was unsuccessful, but experience with JTPA since then has improved knowledge about the use of performance standards in employment and training programs. **CED urges that performance standards be set for the Employment Service, using such measures as placement rates, the wages of those who are placed, the characteristics of those who register with the service, the volume of job orders from employers in the area, and the health of the particular state economy.**

Integration of services with other public employment and training programs also should be considered. At present, the United States does a bad job of making good labor market information available. **The federal government should encourage national job search and worker relocation by providing job seekers in each state with information about openings in other states through the Employment Service.**

RESTRUCTURING WORK

The continuing demand for innovation in an intensely competitive marketplace requires that companies be able to respond quickly and efficiently to changing conditions. This, in turn, requires removing organizational barriers to change. Increasingly, workers are no longer just performing standardized tasks for which they are as interchangeable as the parts they used to assemble. They have become important as individuals because of the new workplace demands for quality, creativity, and flexibility. They can no longer be organized, supervised, evaluated, or rewarded in the old ways if they are to meet these new demands.

The traditional large-scale factory model of organization is breaking down rapidly as individuals and small groups, working with greater independence to accomplish objectives rather than just follow procedures, become increasingly important. Emphasis on the quality rather than the quantity of what is produced necessarily makes individual performance and even self-reliance critical to the overall success of the enterprise. As companies acquire workers with the new kinds of skills discussed earlier

---

PREPARING EMPLOYEES FOR FUTURE EMPLOYMENT: THE FORD-UAW PROGRAM

Faced with long-term declines in productivity and severe global competition, the U.S. auto industry has included comprehensive labor policies in its adjustment strategies. The Ford Motor Company and United Auto Workers (UAW) Joint Employee Development and Training Program articulated a set of principles and established Career Service and Reemployment Assistance Centers in order to meet this challenge. This program was first used when Ford shut down its Hayward, California, assembly plant several years ago, and helped many displaced workers to be retrained and find new jobs in other industries.

The Assistance Centers offer a carefully ordered and comprehensive set of services for Ford employees facing layoffs or job changes. Participants receive help with personal development, including individualized needs assessment and support services for the worker and family when necessary. Career counseling is offered, as well as basic skills training and prepaid tuition assistance at all academic levels. In the training and placement component, the participant can be referred to vocational retraining classes or on-the-job training. Job development resources are also offered, including sessions in job-search skills and placement assistance.

The Ford-UAW centers demonstrate that comprehensive, individualized services can be offered with a long-range view toward lifetime education and career development for the workers.

in this chapter, they will find it increasingly difficult to manage these people in the same old ways. The ability to learn and to excel at tasks, rather than just do what management says, will be the key to job security, which increasingly will be decoupled from long-term dependence on a single employer. This can be seen already in the growing proportion of the work force (now about a quarter) composed of independent contractors, temporary or leased workers, and part-time employees.

Labor-management relations must now support a reorganization of work to increase flexibility and give production workers more control over their tasks. This translates into fewer discrete tasks; the scores of job classifications in typical U.S. manufacturing plants could be replaced by a team system under which everyone is trained to do several jobs (for appropriately higher pay), so that production can be shifted more quickly to meet changing product demands. The skills of all workers need to be integrated into an organization that can absorb shocks and respond to opportunities.

Companies can try to realign their internal organizations to meet the requirements of new technologies and changing market demands by engaging in *productivity bargaining* with their unions. This has typically meant giving workers some financial reward for agreeing to more flexible rules, but the concept could be broadened to include negotiations over obsolete or restrictive management practices.

The aim of all such bargaining should be to produce an adaptive organization that can respond quickly and continuously to changes in product markets and production technologies. Failure to respond to the economic realities of the marketplace is the surest way to make jobs insecure. More openness on the part of management concerning the company's competitive situation could bring about greater willingness on the part of labor to change working arrangements that are hampering the firm's capacity to adapt.

CHANGING PAY PRACTICES

A major part of any strategy to make work and workers more productive is finding better ways to reward individual performance while linking it more directly with the overall success of the firm. Traditional systems of fixed compensation allow employees to view their own pay increases separately from the company's performance. This may have been sustainable in the days of continually growing markets, but in an era of fierce global competition, it is actually hurting workers by forcing employers to adjust to competitive pressures largely by reducing employment.

However, corporate pay practices are changing. A 1985 Conference Board survey found more major companies basing wages on internal criteria such as unit labor costs or profits. This is a significant shift from the earlier practice of patterning increases after those given at other companies in the industry, enshrined in the automobile, steel, and other large manufacturing industries. The survey found, for example, that hourly compensation from 1973 to 1981 rose about as much in industries suffering from declining productivity as it did in those enjoying increases,[8] which probably contributed to the substantial decline in employment in the weaker industries during the 1980s.

Still, it would be unfair to focus exclusively on manufacturing or blue-collar workers. The predominant practice for nearly all employers is to pay people on the basis of what everyone else in their industry is offering, however much may be said about merit pay or pay for performance. Most workers are paid roughly the same as everyone else with the same experience doing the same kind of work in the relevant labor market, regardless of their own or their company's performance.

The movement toward more flexible pay practices must continue if employers are to respond to competitive cost pressures. Nucor Company, a maker of specialty steel faced with strong competition from imports, provides an example of a flexible compensation plan established to help it stay competitive. Nucor ties every employee's compensation to productivity and performance on the job. Base salaries are below the industry's average, but a bonus incentive system can raise these salaries by 50 to 60 percent, depending on the performance of an employee's work team. Compensation varies weekly with business results, giving employees an obvious stake in these results; but the average employee's annual earnings have been consistently higher than those at other steel companies, and no workers have been laid off for fifteen years.

Du Pont's Fibers segment, with annual sales of $6 billion, implemented an Achievement Sharing plan for most of its 20,000 employees in 1989. The plan, which was developed by a special task force after two years of study, seeks to share the department's success with all those responsible for achieving it and supports the changes in corporate culture that promote a more self-directed work force (see page 97).

We would not argue that workers should have major portions of their wages tied to the overall economic performance of their companies. A corporation's earnings are subject to fluctuations for reasons unrelated to any individual employee's performance. Such a policy would make incomes too variable, creating anxiety that would be at cross-purposes with the whole aim of incentive pay, which is to give workers positive inducements to excel at their jobs to the larger benefit of the whole enterprise.

What we are arguing for is a pay system based at least *in part* on real incentives for higher performance, which necessarily means tying part of the reward to the success of the firm as a whole or to the effectiveness of its work units.

At most companies, flexible compensation plans add a group incentive payment to some fixed base, with the amount of the bonus tied to increases in productivity, profitability, or some measure of cost savings. Under a Scanlon plan, for example, so-called *gain-sharing bonuses* are based on a comparison of a plant's payroll costs with the value of its production. Thus, they are based on controlling the direct costs of production, over which workers have much more influence than revenues or profits. Under these plans, which are popular with smaller manufacturing companies, workers' incentive pay depends on the performance of their own work unit, however defined, rather than total company results.

Another form of flexible compensation is *pay for knowledge* or *pay for skills*, whereby employees are paid for learning new skills. General Motors has instituted such a practice at an engine works plant, as part of a new work system built on the concepts of teams, job rotation, and employee participation in decisions about the flow of work (see page 98). In such a setting, the objective of pay for knowledge is to give workers incentives to increase their own ability to perform a larger number of tasks. General Electric also pays workers at some locations for acquiring new skills.

A 1986 Yankelovich survey found that less than a quarter of the workers interviewed believed they were working at their full potential

---

ACHIEVEMENT SHARING AT DU PONT

From the executive vice president on down, 90 percent of the 20,000 employees in Du Pont's Fibers segment will be paid base salaries that are 6 percent below those of other Du Pont workers. If the department meets its profit goal for the year, employees recoup the 6 percent; if profits reach 150 percent of the goal, their pay will be 12 percent higher than that of comparable employees in other departments.

An employee whose base salary was $30,000 prior to Achievement Sharing will now have a base of $28,200. Depending on the department's performance, that figure can rise as high as $33,600.

The department's earnings last year came in $15 million above the goal, and about $10 million was just paid out to workers under the plan.

and that three-quarters thought there was little connection between their pay and their performance. A separate survey by the U.S. Chamber of Commerce discovered that only 9 percent of workers interviewed believed they would benefit from improvement in their firms' productivity, versus 93 percent of Japanese workers.[9]

There is great potential for improving job performance through incentive pay that ties rewards to results. The approaches described here, as well as devices such as employee stock ownership plans and incentive stock options that give workers ownership, can increase individual commitment to the long-term success of a firm. A 1989 survey of 2,000 companies by Mercer Meidinger Hansen found a quarter of them granting stock options or other incentives to middle- or lower-level employees who were previously excluded from such plans. No company has gone farther in this direction than PepsiCo, which now grants stock options to all 100,000 of its employees.

Such a trend would help counter the movement away from personal identification with a particular employer. Most American corporations

---

TEAMWORK AND PAY FOR KNOWLEDGE AT GENERAL MOTORS

When General Motors' Cadillac Motor Car Division moved its Detroit engine works plant to the nearby community of Livonia, the company introduced a new work system built on a concept of team building and employee participation in decision making.

The plant work force, which included 95 percent of the workers from the former site, was divided into fifteen departments and then divided further into work teams of ten to twenty employees. At present, the employees rotate jobs within their teams, fill in for absent coworkers, and explore ways to redesign the work flow for greater productivity. Employees are paid on the basis of the new skills they acquire through a pay-for-knowledge system that provides incentives for them to develop new skills and increase their flexibility at performing a variety of tasks.

The new work system was a significant factor in allowing the Livonia plant to reach the break-even point a full year sooner than anticipated. The plant uses less manpower per engine while increasing product quality. In addition, employees have found that the team system offers them greater opportunities for skills development and decision making within the plant.

have gone to great pains to design elaborate systems of incentives for their executives, including the opportunity to buy stock in the company at favorable prices. If this is indeed one of the ultimate motivators of senior executives, it seems appropriate to ask why the same should not be true for all other employees.

PENSION PORTABILITY

Concern about the continued mobility of the work force as it reaches middle age has led to renewed interest in the portability of pension benefits. The ability to take pension credits or cash values to a new job would facilitate labor market adjustments to changing competitive conditions. Technical issues involved in increasing portability, such as crediting of service between plans and the maintenance of benefit values when changing jobs, are dealt with more easily under defined-contribution rather than defined-benefit plans. A trend is evident toward defined-contribution arrangements, which simplify efforts to change pension policy as well as to maintain the integrity of plans.

Employees who leave companies before meeting vesting requirements usually forfeit all pension benefits. Vesting standards for private employers' defined-benefit plans have now been reduced to a maximum of five years under the Employee Retirement Income Security Act of 1974 (ERISA). One alternative is *graduated vesting,* whereby a worker would gradually become entitled to an increasing portion of a pension benefit as his or her years of service with an employer increased. Graduated vesting also would help to overcome employers' opposition to portability by assuring that they would get some of the economic returns from any investments in training, because employees would have an incentive to remain at least until they were fully vested.

Years of credited service even before vesting are portable under most multiemployer pension plans, which are often defined-contribution rather than defined-benefit arrangements. The current cash values of vested benefits are portable and are often given directly to the employees as lump-sum distributions when they leave. However, these cash-outs are frequently used for current consumption instead of being saved for retirement by transfer into other pension plans or individual retirement accounts (IRAs).[12] In other words, they are treated more like severance pay than portable pension benefits. These distributions are likely to become more common as workers change jobs in response to the change in the law to a five-year vesting standard.

The Employee Benefit Research Institute contends that across-the-board portability of credited service upon changing jobs would be difficult to implement.[13] The value of benefits based on one employer's plan would not necessarily equal the benefit entitlement that would have been earned under another employer's plan because benefit formulas differ widely among plans. And the crediting of nonvested service would be even more difficult.

Current legislative proposals seek to extend the portability of current cash values under both defined-benefit and defined-contribution plans. The change to five-year vesting now makes portability more likely to affect the prime-age cohort of workers as they earn a series of vested benefits during these years because of job changes. To promote the mobility and flexibility of the labor force in responding to the demands of changing competitive conditions, several different approaches have been advanced for assuring that cash distributions are saved for retirement instead of being used for consumption. The recently revived concept of a federal portability agency, first raised twenty-five years ago by a presidential commission, would enable workers changing jobs to deposit any preretirement cash distributions with the agency, which would invest them under the guidance of an independent board of trustees.

Another approach would use existing private financial mechanisms such as IRAs or expanded simplified employee pensions (SEPs) to roll over accrued benefits. A proposal in Congress would provide for group portability pension plans, which would allow employees to transfer any employer distributions as well as their own contributions directly to accounts maintained by pension managers such as banks or insurers. These accounts could also be used to finance retiree health insurance or coverage for long-term care expenses, which are increasingly important employee benefit issues.

INVESTING IN WORKERS' HEALTH

Employers spend more than $100 billion on health care annually, yet, most of them pay very little attention to the actual health of their employees until something goes wrong with it. A small but growing number of companies have instituted corporate wellness or health-promotion programs designed to help keep employees healthy and more productive. An early leader in this field was Kimberly-Clark, with its Health Management Program (see page 101).

Employee assistance programs (EAPs), an outgrowth of occupational alcoholism programs, are now being used by many companies to help workers with a much wider range of health and personal problems. EAPs offer assessment, counseling, and referral to treatment for substance-abuse and mental health problems, as well as counseling for family and marital problems and for financial and legal difficulties. Kimberly-Clark reports that employees who had chemical-dependency problems showed substantial improvements in their job performance and similarly large reductions in absenteeism and on-the-job accidents after using the EAP.

Successful EAPs, like successful wellness programs, should become part of the corporate culture. One of the best programs is Honeywell's, begun a quarter century ago at corporate headquarters and now established at forty locations. At Honeywell, the EAP has two basic purposes: (1) to influence the appropriate use of psychiatric, chemical-dependency, and other services by employees; and (2) to consult with human resources staff and line management concerning the effect of these problems on employees' job performance.

WELLNESS AT KIMBERLY-CLARK

The Health Management Program was begun at the company's headquarters in Dallas more than a decade ago and has since been extended to other locations in response to an awareness of the value of maintaining employees' health. The program incorporates a multidisciplinary approach to wellness, which includes medical screening to assess health risks, occupational health nursing to focus on health promotion and maintenance as well as injury prevention, an employee assistance program to help employees with a variety of personal problems affecting their health and well-being, thirty different exercise classes, and a cardiac rehabilitation program. Other special health-promotion programs have been designed to reduce hypertension, prevent back injuries, manage stress, and control weight.

Kimberly-Clark recognized employee health as a corporate priority and developed this work-site-based program with two objectives in mind: (1) achieving a higher level of health and productivity in its workers; and (2) reducing the rate of increase in its health-care costs. There are no available data concerning the effect on productivity, but the measured health status of employees has improved and the rate of increase in the company's health care costs has slowed. This suggests that the program is succeeding in its aim of producing a healthier work force.

Honeywell is concerned that *too few* employees are using counseling services that could obviate the need for medical care and keep them on the job. The company also believes it can realize greater benefits from more extensive use of treatment for chemical dependency, which accounts for a large share of the program's clients. Data from a comparative study of employees at locations with and without EAPs show psychiatric costs at the EAP sites to be less than half those at the other sites, suggesting how effective these programs can be in resolving workplace problems that impair performance.

A few employers have also recognized the returns to be gained from rehabilitating workers who have suffered disabilities and recapturing the accumulated value of their human capital by returning them to the job. Many disabled employees can be returned to work with limited and inexpensive accommodations in their schedules or duties. Yet, most companies ignore the potential benefits of regaining the lost productivity of experienced employees who want to work. When given the opportunity, disabled employees have repeatedly demonstrated that they can be effective performers again, as Du Pont found from tracking more than 2,700 employees with disabilities over a twenty-five-year span.

A leader in this slowly developing field of disability management is 3M, whose approach grows out of a corporate philosophy emphasizing commitment to its employees as assets rather than expenses. The company has instituted this philosophy at all its facilities, even giving line managers a share of the responsibility for getting their injured workers back on the job.

3M views any employee disability as a serious matter requiring a prompt response followed by continuing attention. The company intervenes quickly after any incidents to assure employees that they are still valued individuals. It then goes to great lengths to get them back to work, preferably at their old jobs or modified versions of them or, if that is not feasible, then at whatever kinds of jobs they can perform. In the process, 3M regains the employees' productivity, keeps their loyalty, and maximizes the return on its human capital investment.

In the maturing labor force of the next decade, with fewer new entrants, employers will have more good reasons to get the most out of their prime-age workers. Wellness programs, EAPs, and active disability management are all examples of ways in which the business community is getting more directly involved in the total lives of employees. These initiatives, like child care and adequate health-care coverage (discussed in Chapters 6 and 8), are part of the business effort that is required to attract and retain a high-quality work force in a changing demographic environment where such workers are likely to be in shorter supply.

Chapter 6

Enlarging the Labor Force

The aging of the U.S. population will put a premium on maximizing the actual labor force participation of all groups of Americans. To respond to the challenge posed by a rising ratio of the elderly to people of working age, this country needs to pull underutilized people into fuller labor force participation.

The underutilized population is diverse. It includes welfare recipients, dislocated workers, at-risk youths, people with disabilities, and working parents. Older Americans are another group with underutilized potential (see Chapter 8). Clearly, these groups overlap, and there are some common problems facing all American workers.

The United States has a flexible, adaptable labor force. As labor markets tighten, they adjust to an altered demographic situation. Within bounds, more workers can be created by improving wages and benefits. This may encourage people who are not working to seek a job, or give an incentive to those working less than full-time to increase their hours. The supply of workers can also be enlarged by changing immigration policies as we recommend in Chapter 7. U.S. employers have other alternatives as well. American companies can go abroad to use foreign labor, and they can substitute capital for labor in their domestic production process. In addition, the United States can import more goods produced abroad by foreign companies and workers. And it can gain additional new workers, many with employable skills, if ongoing changes in the international situation should lead to any substantial demobilization of those now in the armed forces.

Although there is a downside to some of the adjustments needed to increase the supply of future workers, there is also an important opportunity. Tightening domestic labor markets will improve job opportunities for the hard-to-employ in this country.

Our premise is that both the private sector and the government can take steps to facilitate the adjustment process.

RECLAIMING AT-RISK YOUTHS

There is a group of youths in the United States who, for multiple reasons, are at serious risk of becoming permanent dropouts from the larger society. These youths are concentrated in poor families, often headed by a single parent, frequently living in decaying inner-city areas, and beset by a plethora of social problems. Although these youths constitute a distinct minority of total teenagers, they are a critical social problem.

There are perhaps 1 million or more young people facing this plight nationwide. The rationale for concern and intervention lies not only in the moral imperative to take action but also in the fact that this country **needs** all its young people to become a resource, rather than a drain on society. We must develop the skills and motivation of all youths to prepare them for productive working lives.

To reclaim them, we must do several things. We must provide them with better basic academic skills, and that requires keeping them in school. **Business can play an important role here by offering incentives to stay in school, such as the promise of jobs or scholarships for post-secondary education.** Business-education compacts in various cities and the Casey Foundation's New Futures Initiative (see Chapter 3) are examples of such business involvement with education at the community level. **CED urges the formation of more such compacts between business and the public schools to encourage at-risk youths to graduate, upgrade their basic skills for the workplace, and even go on to college.***

Government must also play a role. **The federal government should adequately fund programs such as Chapter One of the Elementary and Secondary Education Act, the Job Training Partnership Act, and the Job Corps** (see Chapter 4). Moreover, state and local governments should integrate and coordinate services to youths in areas ranging from child welfare and health care to job training. All levels of government should reorient programs from after-the-fact crisis management to early intervention.

---

*See memoranda by ELMER B. STAATS (page 163).

Private-sector incentives and government assistance are important, but they cannot do the job by themselves. Young people must be motivated to respond in the desired way. These youths must want to gain and use the skills needed to succeed in the workplace. Yet, they often live in environments that fail to reinforce mainstream values of work, achievement, and self-sufficiency. Incentives cannot work in a vacuum; they must be placed within a supportive culture that reinforces the values to which they are linked.

The fundamental need is to break down the culture of dependency that produces youths at risk. This culture has its deepest roots in a welfare mentality that views people as trapped in poverty. The idea of self-help, of pulling oneself up by the bootstraps, has an honored place in our nation's history. Recently, however, many people seem to have decided that it is not relevant for an "underclass" that can only be pulled out of long-term poverty by others. We believe these youths need ladders, not ropes, so they can climb out under their own power.

Business can help them construct these ladders by providing support and encouragement along with incentives. These young people desperately need to build their self-esteem with the help of caring adults. Mentors can perform this helping role and serve as models to connect the youths to the mainstream culture. **CED urges employers to encourage and help employees and retirees to serve in mentoring programs for at-risk youths.**

A final note is needed here on youths at risk: nowhere is the war against drugs more important than in the urban zones where many of these young people live. Drugs pervade all levels of American society, but these disadvantaged, inner-city youths take the preponderance of deadly street drugs such as crack and are involved in the explosion of violent urban crime. Growing numbers of educated people are turning away from drugs, but this trend is not evident among these young people. At-risk youths come from at-risk families, in which parents are frequently drug users themselves and so hardly suited to educate their children against drugs. This makes the schools a front line in the battle, but the schools must enlist the help of the larger community. This includes business, which can provide the mentors and role models and offer these youths the incentive of part-time or summer jobs if they remain drug free.

REFORMING WELFARE

The U.S. welfare system does not do enough to encourage work. The Family Support Act of 1988 was a step in the right direction; it provided financial incentives for states to move up to 20 percent of their welfare caseloads into employment by 1995. It also improved child-care and Medicaid assistance for working welfare recipients and strengthened enforcement of child support. Government will now pay up to the market rate for child care and will assure up to a year of transitional Medicaid support after a worker has become ineligible for cash assistance under the Aid to Families with Dependent Children (AFDC) program. **States should move quickly to implement the provisions allowing Medicaid to contribute to the worker's share of the cost of private health insurance after the six-month transition during which the worker is fully covered.**

But the welfare reform legislation did not go far enough. Despite a growing body of evidence that job-search assistance and supported work are effective in moving people from welfare to work, these approaches are still underutilized. There is ample evidence that job clubs and job-search assistance, as well as mandatory work requirements for people not taking care of young children, have a positive effect on employment and earnings and reduce public assistance costs. The favorable effects are not overwhelming and are sometimes marginal, but the impact is almost always in the right direction.

CED recommends that states move beyond compliance with the Family Support Act's limited goals to try to place all welfare recipients who can work into jobs. The demographic environment for such an effort is ideal; the tight labor markets we anticipate will create excellent opportunities to place people in jobs.

To give welfare recipients incentives to move from welfare to work, **CED recommends that states make available a wide range of transitional benefits in areas such as child care, transportation, job training, job-search assistance, remedial education, and health care.** The work of the Council of State Community Affairs Agencies in steering poor and hard-to-employ people into mainstream society via jobs is a noteworthy example of promising state-level efforts.

Moreover, the government could take more vigorous action to prevent welfare dependency in the first place. This action could include such measures as expanding the Head Start program, improving the effectiveness of the child welfare system, and targeting JTPA spending more closely to disadvantaged youths facing the greatest difficulties in the labor market. These efforts could also include a federal cash-assistance program to help finance the costs of education and training and reduce school dropout rates. This would be a public-sector complement to the private efforts exemplified by Eugene Lang's I Have a Dream Foundation, which offers youths from inner-city schools in several cities college tuition if they graduate from high school.

SUPPLEMENTING THE EARNINGS OF LOW-WAGE WORKERS

Simply stated, full-time work does not always pay enough to pull people out of poverty. About 6 million poor people live in households where the family's income is below the poverty line even though someone works full-time throughout the year. We believe that as part of a strategy to encourage work effort, a full-time job should become a virtual guarantee of getting out of poverty.

Government can take several different steps to augment the earnings of the working poor. For example, it can provide some type of wage supplement either directly or through tax credits. And child-support enforcement can be made tougher to help single working custodial parents.

There is broad-based support for supplementing the earnings of the working poor by enriching the earned income tax credit (EITC). There are several proposals in Congress to increase the EITC and make it relatively more generous for larger households. **CED recommends an increase in the earned income tax credit as the most direct, effective way to reduce poverty among working Americans.** For example, the EITC could provide a credit equal to 14 percent of earnings for a family with one child, 18 percent for a family with two children, 22 percent for a family with three children, and 26 percent for households with four or more children. In addition, the ceiling on the credit should be raised somewhat from the current level to make it more generous for all recipients. However, these changes should not become so generous that they create disincentives to work over the range of incomes where the tax credit is phasing down, typically about $10,000 to $20,000 a year. The approximate cost to the federal government of the changes in the EITC recommended here would be $3 billion in the first year.

HELPING DISABLED WORKERS

In 1988, an estimated 13.4 million Americans had disabilities that interfered with work. Only about one-third of men and a little over one-fourth of women reporting a work disability were in the labor force in 1988, and their unemployment rates were roughly twice as high as those of nondisabled workers. At the same time, a national survey conducted by the International Center for the Disabled (ICD) found that two-thirds of working-age people (those between the ages of 16 and 64) with disabilities want to work and are less likely to consider themselves disabled if they **are** working. But barriers remain in their way, and some of these have been erected by government programs.

Expenditures for the working-age disabled population exceed $150 billion, largely for income maintenance and medical care; only two to three cents of each dollar go to efforts at rehabilitation and returning these individuals to work.[1] The whole structure of disability benefits acts as a disincentive to rehabilitation and return-to-work efforts. Disability benefits can be inadequate for people who are unable to work because of their age or the severity of their conditions, but Social Security Disability Insurance benefits are nontaxable and they sometimes exceed a worker's prior take-home pay – creating a powerful disincentive to work. The adversarial nature of many workers' compensation cases, pitting injured workers against their employers, is a further obstacle to getting them back on the job.

The experience of Du Pont and other companies has shown that many employees with disabilities are equal or superior to other workers in job performance. Du Pont based this conclusion on studies of 2,750 disabled employees over twenty-five years. Another ICD survey found that nine out of ten managers rated disabled employees good or excellent performers. The Marriott Corporation hires people with disabilities to work in the cafeteria at its corporate headquarters in Bethesda, Maryland. Although Marriott experiences a 105 percent annual turnover rate among its employees in general, the turnover among its workers with disabilities is only 8 percent. The cost per turnover is estimated at $1,500, which is the approximate cost of training a person with disabilities. Moreover, workers with disabilities show 50 percent higher attendance rates, which reduces the cost of paying overtime to those who do the jobs of absent workers. Intangible benefits also accrue to the company in the form of enhanced employee loyalty and conscientious job performance.

The nation is failing to capitalize on the talents of a large group of potential workers who come equipped with a built-in work ethic, even though it often costs little or nothing extra to accommodate individuals with disabilities in the workplace. A U.S. Department of Labor survey of private employers found that more than half of the accommodations for disabled workers cost nothing and that fewer than 10 percent cost more than $2,000. Yet, another survey of major companies found that only 16 percent had return-to-work programs for employees on long-term disability and that only 13 percent offered incentives to get them to return. A quarter of the companies surveyed were planning to revise their long-term disability benefit plans to put more emphasis on managing disability and returning injured workers to their jobs. The time is ripe for employers to do much more.

Corporate policies concerning disability and rehabilitation are shaped by the larger corporate philosophy. Companies that view their employees as assets rather than expenses are likelier to be committed to rehabilitation; this attitude toward workers must come down from top management if it is to permeate the corporate culture, as it does at 3M (see box below).

The keys to successful disability management are early intervention and a commitment to returning the employee to work. Because the time between the injury and referral to rehabilitation is the best predictor of a successful return to work, quick intervention after an injury occurs helps prevent establishment of a "disability syndrome." Coordinated rehabilitation services combined with employers' efforts to make reasonable accommodations for workers with limitations can provide a big payoff in reduced medical costs and income maintenance, as well as reclaimed experience and productivity.

Employers have too often written off disabled workers, choosing to provide compensation and medical benefits as a cost of doing business. But workers' compensation premiums have doubled since 1980, to $35 billion, and this has increased incentives to return disabled workers to the job as

---

DISABILITY MANAGEMENT AT 3M

Instead of the typical employer's hands-off approach to disability, 3M takes an active approach of prompt response, continuing attention, and great effort to get the employee back on the job.

Three principles govern 3M's approach to managing disabilities: (1) early intervention to speed the employee's return to work, (2) emphasis on capabilities rather than limitations, and (3) accountability for benefit costs and management actions.

Line managers are held responsible for managing disability. This is done by charging benefit costs to the employee's department, thereby creating an incentive to enable an early return to work.

The management process is guided by regional coordinators; it features prompt and then regular contact with the treating doctor to track the employee's progress and encourage a return to the job, as well as periodic review and planning to help it along. The first goal is always a return to the same job, modified if necessary to take any limitations into account. Failing this, the company arranges placement in a different position, usually with on-the-job training.

Extra efforts are always made to accommodate the job to the individual's functional capabilities. The most common adjustments are reduced hours or lighter duties, which are gradually increased to reach the goal of a return to a full-time schedule.

quickly as possible. This new focus is now spilling over into private disability plans. **CED urges employers to make rehabilitation and return to work the aim of their disability policies and to use their employee assistance plans to manage disability as well as substance abuse and other personal problems.** Greater labor-management cooperation is also needed to surmount concerns about seniority and transfer rights in returning injured employees to suitable jobs.

Government disability policies should be reformed to complement these private-sector initiatives. Section 1619 of the Social Security Act allows people with disabilities to resume work and retain their benefits for a transitional period. Broadening this concept from cash assistance to health benefits could address the serious problem disabled workers face in maintaining medical insurance. Although they are ineligible for Medicare benefits for a period of two years, they may be excluded from employer-sponsored group health insurance if they return to work. This may encourage them to wait for Medicare benefits to begin or to try to qualify for Medicaid, which is generally difficult for intact families. A better linkage between government health programs and private health insurance is needed here.

ASSISTING DISPLACED WORKERS

Unemployment insurance provides cash benefits for up to twenty-six weeks of unemployment. This system might have been adequate for the traditional layoff, when workers expected to be called back once demand picked up. But in our changing economy, this type of unemployment is being supplanted by the problems of workers who have the wrong skills in the wrong place. Many of these workers have been dislocated by economic change; a few months of benefits will not solve their problem. They need opportunities to be retrained and perhaps to relocate to areas with greater job opportunities. Yet, there is little focus in the unemployment insurance program on reorienting an unemployed worker to a new career or helping that worker to relocate.

CED recommends that a significant amount of unemployment insurance tax revenues be earmarked for retraining and relocation of workers. In the case of relocation, workers should be allowed to take their UI benefits as a front-end lump sum. This step could be taken in a budget-neutral fashion by diverting a portion of federal unemployment tax (FUTA) revenues to retraining.

HELPING WORKING FAMILIES

Various types of family-support policies can make work more attractive and feasible. Many American workers have family responsibilities that compete with full-time labor force participation. There have been extraordinary changes in the American family structure over the past two decades, with dramatic increases in the numbers of dual-income families, single-parent households, and employed women with young children. Employers can be more flexible in accommodating changing family structures, especially the needs of working parents.

The most important component in family policy is child care. It has emerged as an important factor in work force participation and productivity, affecting everyone from the welfare mother who has been retrained and wants to enter the work force to the executive woman who has or wants to have children, and from the divorced father with a joint-custody arrangement to the married father who shares child-care responsibilities with his working wife.

Helping employees care for their children should be seen as part of the compensation package to *attract and retain good workers*. The cost of recruiting and training new workers is very high. Because such a high proportion of new jobs in the future will be filled by women, benefits such as child care and sick-child leave, which have a special appeal for women and, increasingly, for men in the child-rearing years can be especially important in employee recruitment. Given the projected high proportion of women who will fill new jobs (63 percent of new workers from 1986 to 2000), it is not improbable that such benefits should become more commonplace in the future.

Measures that help working parents care for their children can also contribute to *increased productivity* on the job. In the past, the roles of worker and parent were sharply differentiated. Fathers could focus their attention on work because they typically had wives at home to take care of their children, and women who were mothers could focus on child rearing because they typically had husbands whose paychecks covered the family expenses. Today, the roles of worker and parent are often combined, especially for the many women who continue to bear the principal responsibility for child rearing even as they are employed outside of the home.

Parents are constrained in their work roles by the need to ensure that their children are being taken care of. They may resolve conflicts between their jobs and the vicissitudes of school and child-care schedules in favor of their children. When children are sick, when schools are closed, when the child-care provider does not show up, parental responsibilities compete with a worker's responsibility to the job. An estimated 4.5 billion working hours are lost each year because of tardiness, absenteeism, and sickness attributed to problems with fulfilling child-care responsibilities. (Child- care problems cause employees with children under age 13 to lose an average of eight working days a year.) To the extent that employers can help working parents deal with these responsibilities, employees are likely to be both more productive workers and more effective and caring parents. The children of their employees represent an identifiable, finite, and accessible target group to which companies have a clear and practical link.

If the responsibility of employers for giving special concern to the children of their employees could be established as integral to the business and social ethic, the opportunity for generally improving the status of children and young people could be increased significantly. The most significant way in which employers could express such concern for their workers' children – and one that is currently of prime public interest – is helping with child care.

THE NEED FOR CHILD CARE

The average American woman will spend most of her adult life in paid employment and will also bear and raise children. This reality represents the culmination of a long shift in women's work from traditional, unpaid labor in the home to paid labor in the work force. Among women between the typical childbearing years of 25 and 43, 70 percent now have jobs, double the proportion in 1950. This change has brought sweeping consequences for the American family, economy, and workplace.

For the family, it means that nearly two-thirds of households with children under age 18 have mothers in the work force. The most startling increases have occurred among women with very young children. By 1986, over half the women with children younger than 3 and almost 60 percent of those with children under 6 were employed, a 16 percent increase from the previous decade. Approximately 12 million preschool and kindergarten children have working mothers, a figure that is expected to approach 15 million by 1995. Of the jobs created between 1988 and 1995, 67 percent are projected to be filled by women, and it is estimated that 80 percent of the women who take these jobs will become pregnant sometime in their working lives.

These figures do not include the women who would work if they had access to affordable child care. A 1982 Census Bureau survey revealed that 26 percent of nonworking mothers with young children said they would look for work if they could find reasonably priced child care. An additional 13 percent said they would work more hours if cheaper child care were available. Columbia University economist David E. Bloom estimates that if half of the women who say they are constrained by child-care obligations went to work in the 1990s, the labor force would gain 850,000 workers. Moreover, child care is not just a woman's problem; in a recent survey of parents with children under the age of two, 89 percent of women and 62 percent of men reported work-related child-care problems.

Helping employees to obtain *high-quality* child care can yield specific benefits to companies by also helping to attract and retain good workers. It can also help improve the productivity of working parents because convenient and affordable child care can contribute to reducing absenteeism, tardiness, job turnover, and emotional and physical stress.

QUALITY CARE

Working parents seeking high-quality child care quickly learn that much of what is affordable is actually custodial, not developmental, care. Yet, programs that develop children's physical, social, and cognitive skills are what most families want and what experts mean when they talk about "quality care." The National Association of Industrial and Office Parks, which encourages developers to establish child-care centers, has urged its members to use developmental instead of custodial models.

Studies by AT&T and the Adolph Coors Company found that parents have an extremely difficult time finding the kind of care they want. A 1989 Louis Harris poll commissioned by Philip Morris also revealed that fully half of all parents are unhappy with the quality of child care they are buying and stated that Americans overall are concerned about the way children under 6 are cared for while their parents work.

For most American families, child care is made up of a hodgepodge of stable and makeshift arrangements. Families piece together packages of care depending on their budgets and work schedules and on their children's ages, health, and school schedules. The more numerous the arrangements, the more often they break down. Various studies show that child-care plans fall through an average of three times a year for women and two-and-a-half times a year for men and that children under 12 become sick an average of five days a year.[2]

Not surprisingly, parent-employees report extraordinary stress related to child-care troubles. The degree of difficulty in finding child care is one of the most significant predictors of absenteeism, according to a 1986 *Fortune* magazine study conducted by Bank Street College and the Gallup organization. Approximately one in four workers is taking a less demanding job or refusing a promotion because of child-care concerns, the study said. Aetna Life & Casualty Insurance Co. revamped its personnel policies to provide more flexible working arrangements after discovering that 21 percent of the women who left technical positions did so because of family obligations. A 1988 member survey by the National Association of Business Women found that 65 percent of those with children believed they could assume additional responsibilities or higher level jobs if they had better child care.

Many companies still find it hard to justify assisting their workers with child care. They view the costs as prohibitive or not worth the benefit, fear liability, anticipate resentment from employees without children, resist the diversion from mainstream business concerns, and are hesitant to introduce a new and potentially complex and costly benefit.[3] All these concerns are understandable.

Still, many companies have concluded that the pressures for dealing with the issue of child care are unavoidable and that the benefits exceed the costs. At present (in 1990), about 5,400 companies with 100 or more employees offer child-care benefits ranging from financial assistance to direct provision of child care either at or near the work site.[4] This represents a dramatic increase from 110 employers in 1978 and only 600 employers in 1982.

Surveys indicate that managers believe the 70 to 90 percent of the firms that do provide child-care services are more competitive in recruiting workers and have less employee turnover, fewer job-related accidents, less absenteeism, and greater productivity.[5] Moreover, studies by several large corporations, including IBM, Merck, and Corning Glass, show that family responsibilities often contribute to reduced performance, higher turnover, greater absenteeism, and worsening health among workers. Companies also are adversely affected when experienced employees turn down transfers or promotions because they cannot reconcile work and family responsibilities.[6]

AFFORDABLE CARE

Quality child care is unaffordable for some families and in short supply in some areas. The quality of care is uneven and difficult for people to ascertain in advance. Consequently, there is a need not only to help working parents pay for child care but also to increase the supply of quality care available to them.

People who can pay for child care themselves should do so, and they should be able to select their own care, free from overly restrictive government regulation. Finding and paying for child care are primarily the responsibilities of the family, not of government or the employer. Nonetheless, both government and business can help. Government can provide financial aid to lower-income households that could not afford child care on their own or create an infrastructure to support the delivery of care. Business can facilitate child care in a variety of ways.

For most working families, child care is the fourth most expensive budget item, after food, housing, and taxes.[7] The average cost of care per child is $3,000, but actual expenses can be much higher in major urban areas. Moderate child-care costs can easily consume 20 to 30 percent of the family budget when two infants or preschoolers are involved. The financial burden is particularly high for single mothers; whereas the cost of care per child represents about 10 percent of a two-earner family's budget, it represents 25 percent of a single mother's.[8]

The poor pay of child-care workers has been holding costs down, but this also explains much of the unsatisfactory quality and inadequate supply of care. Child-care workers are among the lowest-paid 10 percent of wage earners; 60 percent earn no more than $5 an hour. Turnover is very high (at least 40 percent) because of the low pay, poor benefits, unregulated working conditions, and poor prospects for training and advancement. This situation may worsen as the labor market tightens and women, who are the majority of child-care providers, opt for better-paid jobs.

Policy initiatives to improve the quality of child care should address the need to offer competitive wages and benefits for child-care providers. Massachusetts, for example, raised the average annual salary of child-care workers in centers that receive state aid to nearly $17,000. However, higher compensation would drive up costs, making child care unaffordable for more low-income families. This dilemma heightens the need to carefully target public subsidies to help reconcile the goals of quality and affordability for lower-income working parents.

OPTIONS FOR BUSINESS

To attract and retain workers today and to help raise a sound generation of workers for tomorrow, American employers should increase their involvement in child-care assistance programs. Employers that want to help with child care for their employees can choose from an array of options ranging from increasing the availability of information to increasing the supply of services and providing more flexible personnel

116

and benefit policies. Others can contribute to community agencies to improve overall services and can make their internal policies more responsive to employee needs.

Whatever shape they take, assistance efforts should not try to dictate solutions. Rather, they should focus on expanding employees' options by filling gaps in the existing child-care network.

The following sections describe several ways in which businesses can assist employees in getting convenient, affordable, high-quality child care.

RESOURCE AND REFERRAL PROGRAMS

In 1986, there were 40,000 licensed day-care centers in the United States. **Businesses could help their employees find and select appropriate child care by providing them with information and counseling. Educating employees to be effective consumers of child care is one way of increasing the likelihood that their children will get quality care.** This option could help reduce absenteeism and increase productivity by improving employee child-care arrangements. Employers can designate or hire an in-house specialist or contract with an outside consultant to develop these services. Currently, 1,500 companies offer their employees referral services. Thousands more offer counseling, parenting seminars, support groups, libraries, newsletters, handbooks, hotlines, and caregiver fairs.

Large companies with offices scattered throughout a region or the nation sometimes contract with an outside consultant or organization to provide child-care information by telephone or even subcontract with local agencies that monitor child-care services. IBM created a national contractor in Watertown, Massachusetts, called Work/Family Directions, Inc., to identify and, sometimes, help create local resource and referral programs for employees at its 200 sites. Work/Family Directions now serves 40 companies across the country, using a network of about 300 local resource and referral subcontractors. Employees who need child care notify the local subcontractor, who functions as a "search counselor," comparing parents' needs with what is available and providing them with legal and educational information.

The Child Care Coordinating Council of Portland, Oregon, is a computerized child-care information and referral system initiated by the City Club of Portland and financed by local businesses. A City Club study found that more than 60,000 children would benefit if better information about services were available. The council computerizes information about specific services and costs and matches them with parent inquiries.

Resource and referral programs can reduce the amount of time employees spend searching for child care. However, such programs are ultimately limited by the quantity and quality of the local supply of care unless employers take steps to increase that supply and improve quality.

ADAPTABLE PERSONNEL POLICIES

Many working parents find it difficult to reconcile the demands of their work schedules and the schedules of their children's schools and day-care centers. To help ease this problem, **employers can arrange for more flexible work schedules.** Options include:

- **Flextime,** which permits employees to determine when to start and end their workday within some broad bands of time

- **Compressed time,** such as four 10-hour days rather than five 8-hour days

- **Part-time work,** less than the standard work week, but on a permanent basis with regular, prorated benefits

- **Job sharing,** where two or more employees share responsibility for the same job

- **Home work and task contracting,** where employees are assigned specific tasks to be completed at a given time and date but can perform them when and where they choose

To the extent that these options relieve parents of the stress and time constraints associated with conventional work schedules, they could increase employee productivity. As a practical matter, however, there are likely to be costs and complications involved in facilitating more flexible scheduling. Firms and workers will have to find the proper degree of flexibility in work schedules that balance their respective needs. Such policies do not obviate the need for child care so much as facilitate parents' scheduling an appropriate combination of arrangements for their children.

FLEXIBLE BENEFITS

Companies can also provide child-care assistance as part of their benefit packages. There are several options, the costs of which vary considerably:

- **Cafeteria benefits:** Child care might be provided as one of the optional benefits in a flexible or cafeteria-style benefit package.

- **Salary reduction for tax purposes:** Federal tax laws permit families to divert up to $5,000 of their pretax wages to cover dependent-care costs. Technically, their salaries are reduced, and the company pays for their child-care costs.

- **Payment by the firm:** Firms can choose to pay all or part of an employee's child-care costs.

When firms help pay for child care, they may also seek a role in determining what kind of care the employee chooses to purchase with this benefit. In some instances, for example, they might limit the choice of

---

FLEXIBLE BENEFIT AND PERSONNEL POLICIES AT STEELCASE, INC.

Steelcase, Inc., a large office furniture maker, has pioneered in the development of innovative approaches to child-care assistance for employees since 1979, when it began a program to train women to become home day-care providers. In the past decade, the Grand Rapids, Michigan, company has become one of the few major American corporations to implement a range of flexible benefit and personnel options to help its 8,000 employees meet family obligations. Roughly 400 of Steelcase's 2,000 office workers are on flextime, including 40 who share 20 jobs. In addition, all employees, including the 6,000 factory workers, choose from a cafeteria-style program offering the standard benefits as well as extras, such as tax-free spending accounts for child care.

Choice and flexibility are the hallmarks of Steelcase's programs. The benefit policy allots employees "benefit dollars" that they can spend as they choose and allows them to change their choices (with some restrictions) as their needs change. Tax-free money set aside for child care can be switched to meet health care or retirement needs, or vice versa. With careful planning, working couples can eliminate unneeded or duplicate coverage and bring home unused benefit dollars as cash. The company believes that it benefits, too, by saving money on rising costs for insurance plans that employees may not want or need.

Flextime and job-sharing policies enable employees to work unconventional hours, a boon for the company as well as for workers with young children. Managers claim that liberalized personnel practices have reduced absenteeism among working mothers and note that most job sharers eventually return to full-time employment. The program has been so successful that a pilot has been started for some of the 6,000 factory workers.

Steelcase believes that its personnel and benefit policies help to maximize profits, morale, and productivity and to minimize turnover. Indeed, its annual turnover rate is a remarkably low 3 percent, compared with an average 18 percent rate nationally for all occupations.

providers to those believed to offer the kind of quality care that will play a positive role in the child's development. Steelcase, Inc., a Michigan-based office furniture company, has recruited 350 licensed home-based providers for its employees as part of a program that features flexibility and choice (see page 118).

Of all forms of employer-supported child-care assistance, flexible benefit plans with dependent-care options have multiplied the fastest because they offer both employers and employees the greatest degree of choice. For example, two-earner families can avoid duplicative and unnecessary health-care coverage while obtaining tax-free child-care services. Employers can control or reduce benefit costs and pay lower Social Security and unemployment taxes.

Well-known employers with flexible benefit programs, in addition to Steelcase, include the Educational Testing Service, Harvard University, Primerica, Procter & Gamble, General Foods, Chemical Bank, Zayre, Polaroid, and PepsiCo.

COMPANY-SUPPORTED CHILD-CARE FACILITIES

Firms can also choose to operate or contract out their own child-care facilities for employees. They may, for example, establish a full-service center on or near the work site. It might be operated by the firm, by a consortium of employers, or by an outside organization. Employers may pay some of the costs, and they may also provide various in-kind or free facilities. Children of nonemployees might also be accepted.

Employer-created child-care centers, either at or near the workplace, have won the most visibility and publicity for companies and are highly appreciated by employees. Half of all parents prefer on-site care, especially for young children, according to a national study by the Carnegie Corporation.

Facilities organized by the firm and located near the place of work make it convenient for employees to drop off and pick up children, and it is reassuring for them to have their children nearby. For the children, the benefits include quality care and the reassurance of knowing that their parents are nearby and often able to visit them during the day. For the firm, on-site or nearby facilities are the most likely to enhance recruitment and retention. A policy of allowing workers to visit their children on breaks could also ease parents' concerns, thereby improving their concentration and productivity. Another benefit for the firm lies in being able to control the quality of the facility, thereby ensuring that children are getting good care.

The Stride Rite Corporation opened one of the first company-sponsored child-care centers in 1971 in the Boston area. Its two centers now enroll about 100 preschoolers, about half of them the children of employ-

120

ees. Each center costs about $325,000 a year to operate, and the Massachusetts Department of Social Services contributes to the cost. Employees pay varying fees up to 14 percent of their salaries to enroll their children; Stride Rite contributes the balance, which is about $200,000 per year.

Other employers that have established successful centers include Hartz Mountain, Campbell Soup, Rouse & Associates, Corning Glass, Trammell Crow, and Lancaster Laboratories (see boxes this page and 121). Stride Rite has put its experience to work helping to develop 50 centers around the country. And the United Auto Workers and Chrysler Corporation recently announced plans to develop and jointly operate an on-site

HARTZ MOUNTAIN, INC. AND HARMONY EARLY LEARNING CENTER

Since it opened in 1987 to serve the expanding corporate residential communities in the Hackensack Meadowlands area of northern New Jersey, the Harmony Early Learning Center has been caring for about 130 infants, preschoolers, and kindergartners a day.

The center is the product of a unique three-pronged private- and public-sector response to a development commission's determination that a child-care facility was needed. Hartz Mountain Industries, Inc., a multimillion dollar producer of pet products that is based in the area, donated the land and constructed the 10,000-square-foot building. Hartz then leased the building for $1 annually for ten years to Meadowlands Ministries, Inc., an interdenominational organization of six religious groups that operates the center. In addition, nearly $400,000 in monetary and in-kind gifts for start-up and ongoing operating costs has been contributed by other companies and leaders in the community.

Open from 7:30 A.M. to 6:30 P.M., the center cares primarily for children from 6 weeks of age through kindergarten but also operates a summer program for school-age children. The state-licensed facility requires that its caregivers have state teaching licenses. Fees range from $95 to $142 a week; the younger the child, the higher the cost. Scholarships are available and are supplemented by fund-raising efforts. Parents are free to drop by and visit their children at any time for any reason. Using a developmental approach, with activities that cultivate children's language, physical, and social skills, the center sees its purpose as offering "young children and their families support; appropriate emotional, social, physical, and intellectual development; and quality caregiving in a safe, loving, and nurturing environment."

child-care center for employees at Chrysler's plant in Huntsville, Alabama. Hundreds of employers have been able to reduce start-up and operating costs through public-private partnerships or by forming consortiums with other employers (see page 122). The state of New Jersey, which headquarters a growing number of large corporations and launched an aggressive public-private child-care initiative in 1982, now houses about 100 of the approximately 800 employer-supported centers that exist nationwide.

With 37 percent of the nation's preschoolers being cared for in homes, family child-care networks are particularly popular. The Neighborhood Child-Care Initiatives Project, funded by American Express with additional support from Chase Manhattan Bank and Manufacturers Hanover, identifies potential community network sponsors and helps them with

---

LANCASTER LABS

Lancaster Laboratories, Inc., a relatively small private firm with 300 employees, converted some old corporate offices into a twenty-eight-unit child-care center in 1986 and opened a newly constructed facility in 1988. The on-site center in Leola, Pennsylvania, cares for over 100 children from the age of 2 months through kindergarten and is certified to serve children up to age 12. Special summer and before- and after-school programs exist for school-age children, as does an hourly, emergency drop-in service. About a third of the slots are reserved for Lancaster's employees (the rest are open to the community), who enjoy a 20 to 30 percent discount from fees that range from $51 to $72 a week, with the youngest children costing the most. The center is operated by Magic Years, the largest for-profit child-care provider in Pennsylvania, which operates twenty-seven licensed centers in the state.

Why did Lancaster Labs, an independent provider of chemical and biological services to food, environmental, and pharmaceutical companies, invest significant resources in on-site child care? According to its president, Dr. Earl H. Hess, corporate demographic data showed a conclusive need. With 32.1 the average age of the firm's employees, surveys showed that a large percentage of those who did not already have children planned to start families within five years. Two-thirds of employees are women, and they belong to two-career families. "LLI wanted to make it easier for a person to maintain both a family and a career," Dr. Hess says. "The success of this venture, by whatever yardstick you choose, has been immeasurable." The benefits for LLI have included improved recruiting, reduced turnover, and extremely positive community relations.

recruitment and training. The project, coordinated by Child Care Inc., has so far helped recruit and train 400 women to be family day-care providers in New York City. Employers can also consider less formal measures. For example, they could set aside a "kids' room" in or near the workplace where employees could bring their children on an emergency basis or when they are too sick to go to school but well enough to accompany their parents to work. Alternatively, a firm might permit parents to bring sick children to a company infirmary.

NEW YORK CITY WORK & FAMILY CORPORATE CONSORTIUM

Claiming that American businesses lose $3 billion a year to child-care-related absences, seven New York City-based companies formed the Work & Family Corporate Consortium to conduct a feasibility study and then launch an innovative emergency child-care service. (Participating corporations include Colgate-Palmolive, Home Box Office Inc., Time Inc. Magazines, and Warner Communications Inc.) With a pilot program launched in September 1989, the service is helping employees of the firms when their children become ill, regular child-care plans fall through, or work obligations require travel or irregular hours. The program will serve well and sick children and will meet the twenty-four-hour and overnight needs of working parents.

The service will be available to children of employees who live in the five boroughs of New York City and four counties in northern New Jersey. Besides paying for the actual service, each company will pay a coordination fee of $3,000 to Child Care Inc., the non-profit organization that conducted the feasibility study and will administer the service. Child Care Inc. has contracted with two home day-care agencies to provide the actual emergency caretakers and hopes to expand its network of contracted agencies during the first year. Each participating company will develop its own internal financing options but will subsidize the service in whole or in part.

The feasibility study conducted for the consortium by Child Care Inc. surveyed sick-care programs around the country and factored in the New York City area's unique needs. The study recommended an emergency **in-home** care service because of the popularity of in-home care, especially for sick children, and the high cost of center-based care in Manhattan.

Employers that have developed some form of child-care assistance have almost unanimously concluded that the costs are more than offset by the savings in other areas. An analysis of six studies by Dana Friedman, co-president of the Families and Work Institute, suggests that the biggest gains are in improved recruitment and reduced turnover. Similarly, the National Employer-Supported Child-Care Project, a study conducted in 1982 with results published in 1984, surveyed 178 American companies that provided some form of child-care assistance, ranging from information services to actual care centers. These companies reported a 50 to 90 percent improvement in ten key areas, especially recruitment, morale, and favorable publicity. The other areas were turnover, productivity, worker satisfaction, lateness, absenteeism, motivation, and community relations.

GOVERNMENT ASSISTANCE FOR CHILD CARE

The federal government spends about $7 to $8 billion today on child care, much of it not well-targeted to financial need. The biggest federal effort is the child- and dependent-care tax credit; the revenue loss resulting from this credit is now around $4 billion. About half of the credit's benefits flow to upper-income families; in 1985, nearly 2 million claimants lived in households with $40,000 or more in annual income.

This tax credit is not only uncapped but also nonrefundable. Consequently, although it provides benefits to many affluent families, it offers no help to the working poor who have no federal tax liability. The federal government also provides assistance for child care, directly or indirectly, through the Social Services Block Grant program (Title XX of the Social Security Act), Head Start, and the Child-Care Food Program. The food program, a part of the National School Lunch Act, provides funding to child-care centers and family and group day-care homes to cover the cost of meals and snacks for children. Other federal programs with a child-care component include AFDC, JTPA, and the Community Development Block Grant.

TARGETING AID TO NEED

The first step in reforming government policy is to target current public-sector funding more on the basis of financial need. **CED recommends capping the child-care and dependent-care tax credit and using the revenue gain to help low-income families.** The additional revenue might be used, for example, to expand the Head Start program, which currently serves only about one out of five children who are eligible.

Another alternative is to provide these funds directly to lower-income parents to use in arranging child care. This might be achieved by using the money to fund part of the earned-income tax credit enrichment or the special tax credit for parents with a child under 6, both of which are currently under consideration in Congress.

CED believes that government policy should not favor one type of child care over another, as long as the care is of good quality. The federal government should not add a new layer of regulatory requirements. Regulation of child-care facilities, which is best done at the state and local levels of government, should promote safety and health for children without requiring that caregivers have more credentials than necessary or saddling providers with unnecessary requirements.

STATE CHILD-CARE INITIATIVES

State governments have been very active in recent years in encouraging the provision of child care. Some of these initiatives involve state tax incentives for business, in addition to direct state assistance programs. For example, the large number of employer-supported child-care centers in New Jersey is the result of an aggressive public-private effort launched by the state in 1982. In that year, with just seven such centers in the state, former Governor Thomas H. Kean convened a conference of business executives "to emphasize to the corporate sector the important role of child care as a means of helping New Jersey's economy." He then designated a top official in the state's Division of Youth and Family Services (DYFS) to serve as "a one-stop information resource" on employer- supported child care and to develop, coordinate, and disseminate information, technical assistance, and support efforts.

In conjunction with the state's Division of Women, DYFS established the Task Force on Child Care and the statewide Child Care Clearinghouse. The state has responded to hundreds of calls for assistance, over half from private employers and 80 percent of these from small businesses. It has also established four child-care centers for state employees.

New Jersey is not the only state that has been active in this field. A National Conference of State Legislatures study of public-private child-care partnerships found a dramatic increase in state legislation enacted between 1984 and 1987 and directed at child-care providers and the community at large. Thirteen states currently offer tax incentives to private employers for child-care programs, with the most activity in Connecticut, Rhode Island, and Oregon. California enacted an employer-assisted child-care tax credit in 1988 with provisions that encourage employer investment in both start-up and ongoing efforts.

Development and land-use requirements in California and Maryland stipulate that new state buildings allocate space for child care. San

Francisco went farther, passing an ordinance in 1985 that requires office and hotel developers constructing an addition of at least 50,000 square feet to set aside on-site or off-site child-care space or to contribute to the city's Affordable Child-Care Fund.

FAMILY LEAVE

In recent years, there has been growing interest in the issue of parental leave. In the United States, the issue of how much time off a new parent may take and still retain the same job has been left to the judgment of management and labor. Many large firms have liberal leave policies for new mothers, but most small firms are unable or unwilling to guarantee a job for an extended period when a female employee has a child. There is no government standard requiring employers to grant a minimum leave of absence. In contrast, most other industrial nations assure at least two or three months of leave. Some countries guarantee workers much longer periods at home (e.g., nine months), and workers receive leave with pay. The United States is groping for a policy that protects the job rights of all new parents who are working and assures them of an opportunity to spend time with their newborn without imposing unacceptable costs on employers. A promising development in five states is the establishment of temporary disability insurance plans that provide wage replacement at little cost to employers or employees.

Various proposals have been put forward that would require employers to provide unpaid family or medical leave when an employee becomes a new parent. These proposals extend such leave for a few months with protection of employment rights and employee benefits. In addition to proposals at the federal level, thirteen states have passed parental-leave legislation, and thirty states have such legislation pending.

Generally speaking, employers will often find it in their self-interest to provide some sort of job and benefit security to new parents. In the emerging demographic and labor market conditions that we foresee, most firms will certainly not want to encourage turnover. The modern family typically must juggle work and parental responsibilities and is trying to find a proper balance. The weeks immediately following the birth of a child are a time when at least one working parent needs to be at home nurturing the infant.

By the same token, flat rules and requirements of the sort that emerge from government mandates can impose significant costs for some firms, particularly small ones. (It should be noted here that family-leave proposals typically provide an exemption for firms below a certain work-force size threshold.)

We oppose legislatively mandated approaches to parental leave, which tend to impose arbitrary and costly requirements on business. But we urge employers to institute their own family-leave policies suited to their own circumstances. This would obviate inappropriate mandates while enhancing the well-being and productivity of their employees.

ELDER CARE

The family is the primary source of care for the elderly who need assistance at home. Nearly three-quarters of frail older persons depend on a combination of family care and paid help. Care-giving can be stressful for family members who must also maintain other family and work responsibilities. The typical caregivers are adult daughters, often in their forties and fifties, an increasing number of whom are working. These include the "sandwich generation," which is caring for both aging relatives and their own children. Younger adult caregivers are less likely to live in the same neighborhood or even the same metropolitan area as their parents and therefore are less able to provide care when their parents come home from the hospital.

Corporations are becoming cognizant of the problems encountered by their employees who are caring for elderly family members. One study estimated the cost of lost work time attributed to caring for an aged parent at $2 million for a 25,000-person work force. The Travelers Companies found that one out of every five employees over age 30 provides some care to an elderly parent. The employees have, on average, been providing care for about ten hours a week for five and a half years; 8 percent of them provide more than thirty-five hours of care a week. Moreover, of the elderly parents, 35 percent live a substantial distance from the employee, which complicates the care-giving.

A survey of the members of the New York Business Group on Health showed that companies are aware of the effects of such responsibilities on employee productivity. Of the sixty-nine respondents, about 70 percent reported that lateness and absenteeism were problems, and 60 percent observed excessive stress and physical complaints among the caregivers.

Some companies have concluded that it is in their interest to help their employees help elderly family members. As in the case of child care, options for business involvement include information and counseling to help employees negotiate and arrange for social and health services, flexible work hours, and more direct involvement. Con Edison, Mobil, and Ciba-Geigy conducted a series of seminars for their employees on the services that are available to provide respite care. Travelers, after reviewing its own survey results, is planning to allow employees to take a combination of paid and unpaid leave to care for sick relatives. The company will also provide a referral service and financial subsidies for elder care. Stride Rite Corporation will provide services directly through an on-site intergenerational day-care center for employees' children *and* parents.

Unions are also involved in elder care, and are working with companies to bring help to employees with heavy family responsibilities. The International Ladies Garment Workers Union, for example, has a long-standing program under which retired union members serve as "friendly visitors" to other retirees requiring assistance with daily living.

Clearly, business support for elder care will become more important in the years ahead. As this issue comes to rival child care in urgency for working caregivers, flexible leave policies introduced to deal with child-care needs will be extended gradually to the care of older dependents.

A NEW DIMENSION TO HUMAN RESOURCE MANAGEMENT

A few large employers around the United States are recognizing the greater importance of family issues by creating a new position within the corporate hierarchy to help employees manage the conflicts between the responsibilities of the home and the workplace. For example, Du Pont's director of work force partnering handles these issues and affirmative action as well. Titles such as "family issues coordinator" and "program manager of work/life issues strategy" are appearing on corporate rosters.

Whatever these new corporate professionals are called, they have two important roles: (1) to alter their employers' traditional aversion to getting involved in employees' personal lives off the job and (2) to help shape effective policies for dealing with employee family responsibilities. More companies are finding that it makes good business sense to ensure that their employees' work and family obligations are in harmony instead of pulling in different directions.

AT&T is one of these companies. It now has a manager of work/ family issues who is responsible for a ten-part work and family benefits program agreed on by the company and the Communications Workers of America last year. This agreement is widely regarded as a major step in addressing work and family concerns. Its centerpiece is a $10 million fund for child care and elder care. Joint worker-management committees were established to review and implement employee suggestions on how to spend these dollars. The contract also introduced unpaid leaves for up to a full year for new parents and workers who have dependents with serious illnesses.

One analyst of work and family issues concludes that business is now moving beyond awareness to action, introducing new programs and policies and putting someone in charge of them. Although only a handful of pioneers have acted so far, they have opened a new frontier in human resource management, and others can be expected to follow soon. However, it should also be recognized that the cost of such flexibility can be prohibitive for very small employers when key workers are involved.

* * *

Government should do a better job of providing both a safety net and a front-end boost for lower-income households. In areas such as cash assistance, Medicaid, and child care, many people living in poverty go without needed government help, *often because they are working*. Government financial aid should be better targeted to need rather than working status and should certainly *not penalize* people *for working*.

Finally, there is a danger that government will *overregulate* social services. This occurs now in the case of state health benefit mandates and is in danger of happening in the case of child and elder care. Scaling back such regulation, combined with well-targeted financial assistance, are two prongs of an effective government strategy to empower people to select the social services they need to participate actively in the labor force.

Chapter 7

The Role of Immigration in Meeting Work Force Needs

Immigration historically has played a vital role in shaping American culture and has contributed to the diversity and flexibility of the American work force. We believe that this will continue to be the case in the future. Indeed, with a more slowly growing population, we are moving into a period of skill shortage in which we should be even more open to immigration.

Although immigration has always helped to meet the nation's labor needs, current immigration policies have been shaped largely by noneconomic factors, such as support for family reunification. Our immigration policies, like other policies that affect the work force, need to be adjusted to changing circumstances.

Fortunately, the conditions likely to prevail in the coming years should permit us to increase overall immigration and thereby expand our ability to accommodate family reunification, refugees, and foreign policy concerns even as we place relatively greater emphasis on the economic implications.

Note: *This chapter draws on a background paper by Kevin McCarthy and Georges Vernez of the RAND Corporation, "Meeting the Economy's Labor Needs Through Immigration: The Rationale and the Challenges." However, neither RAND nor the authors of that paper are responsible for the policy recommendations made in this statement.*

We should also recognize that the long-term economic and demographic trends creating a tighter labor market for key skills affords an opportunity to deal with some of the country's most serious social problems because these conditions create greater incentive to train and hire the hard-to-employ. Consequently, although we should both increase the overall magnitude of immigration and adjust the mix to reflect the new economic and demographic realities, we must do so in a way that accommodates and supports efforts to bring the hard-to-employ into the work force.

A comprehensive and balanced immigration policy should address four basic questions: (1) How many immigrants should be admitted each year? (2) What combination of individual characteristics should immigrants have? (3) What occupational, sectoral, locational, and/or other restrictions (if any) should be placed on each individual immigrant? and (4) How long should each immigrant be allowed to stay in the country (i.e., permanently or temporarily)?

To address these questions properly requires consideration of the outlook for forces shaping immigration; the economic consequences of immigration policy, including the possible displacement of native-born workers by immigrants; social issues; and foreign policy implications.

THE OUTLOOK FOR IMMIGRATION

Demand for immigration to the United States is likely to increase for a number of reasons. First, the demographic pressures and slow economic growth in Third World countries will continue to spur outmigration for many years to come. During the next twenty years, the work force in Third World countries is projected to increase by some 700 million people. Unless those countries can substantially increase their rates of economic growth and job creation, many of those new workers will not find employment at home and will seek to emigrate to the United States and elsewhere. Figure 11 shows the wide disparity in projected population growth among nations. Second, the large earnings differentials between the United States and most other countries are likely to remain a potent motivation for emigration even if there are enough jobs in these lower-wage countries. Third, political changes and instability are likely to continue generating a large number of refugees and emigrants. Fourth, other industrialized countries have become increasingly restrictive in their immigration policies, so the United States will be the most likely country of destination for would-be immigrants. Fifth, the dramatic growth in the

131

FIGURE 11

Projected Population Growth Rates Among Nations, Annual Averages, 1986 to 2000 (percent)

Above 3%	Rate	1% to 2%	Rate
Kenya	3.9%	Australia	1.9%
Saudi Arabia	3.8	Ireland	1.0
Tanzania	3.4	Hong Kong	1.0
Nigeria	3.3		
Pakistan	3.0	**0% to 1%**	
		Cuba	0.8
2% to 3%		Canada	0.7
		USSR	0.7
Algeria	2.9	United States	0.6
Bolivia	2.6	Japan	0.5
Vietnam	2.4	France	0.4
Philippines	2.3	Spain	0.4
South Africa	2.3	Italy	0.1
Mexico	2.1	United Kingdom	0.1
		East Germany	0.0
1% to 2%		Sweden	0.0
Brazil	1.9		
India	1.8	**Less than 0%**	
Indonesia	1.8		
Thailand	1.6	Austria	-0.1
China	1.4	Belgium	-0.1
Chile	1.2	Denmark	-0.1
Korea, Republic of	1.2	Hungary	-0.1
Argentina	1.1	West Germany	-0.3

SOURCE: The World Bank, *World Development Report 1988*, (Washington, D.C.: Oxford University Press, 1988), Table 27.

number of foreigners temporarily studying or working in the United States creates a large pool of would-be permanent immigrants.

The impact of these forces on the U.S. labor market is particularly vivid in California. Between 1970 and 1980, California added about 310,000 new jobs annually. If job growth had continued at the same rate throughout the 1980s and the state's 15- to 24-year-olds had entered the labor market at the same rate as their predecessors a decade earlier, California would have faced a shortage of approximately 80,000 workers simply because the potential supply of native-born new entrants to the labor force declined sharply. In fact, although labor markets in California have tightened during the 1980s and wages rose accordingly, the situation did not reach crisis proportions for a number of reasons, including an increase in native-born employment due to higher employment rates among women and older workers. But the continued influx of immigrants into the labor market played a critical role; immigrants contributed more than 25 percent of California's employment growth.

Current U.S. immigration policy seeks to balance four main objectives: (1) to reunite families, (2) to address the labor needs of the economy by admitting permanent or temporary workers, (3) to resettle refugees and accept those seeking asylum for humanitarian and foreign policy reasons, and (4) to facilitate economic and cultural exchanges with other nations. In general, immigrants fall into one of four categories: lawful, permanent immigrants; temporary immigrants or workers; illegal immigrants; and refugees.

Currently, family reunification is the dominant criterion for legal permanent entry into the United States. There are no limits on the number of parents, spouses, or minor children of U.S. citizens that may be permitted to enter the country, although specified annual ceilings are placed on other relatives. In the aggregate, immigrants are subject to a worldwide ceiling of 270,000 visas annually, a per-country ceiling of 20,000 visas annually, and the specific requirements in one of six preference categories, each limited by a specific ceiling. Four of the preference categories emphasize family reunion and account for 80 percent of all visas under the worldwide ceiling. The remaining 20 percent (54,000 annually) are split between members of the professions and workers in occupations in short supply in the United States.

Most temporary visitors to the United States are here for tourism, but some 3 million people enter the country every year to work or perform services for a specified period of time. About two-thirds of these people are here to arrange commercial transactions that do not involve gainful employment in the United States. The Immigration Reform and Control Act (IRCA) established the Replenishment Agricultural Worker (RAW) program, which allows for the legal *temporary* entrance of agricultural workers in numbers determined by the Department of Labor in consultation with the Department of Agriculture.

Illegal immigrants include not only those who enter the country without visas but also "overstayers" who enter the country legally but stay in this country beyond the period specified by their visas. Illegal immigration is estimated by the U.S. Bureau of the Census to be running at a historically high level of about 200,000 people a year. Efforts to restrict the flow of illegal immigrants have had limited success. Extremely rapid growth of the working-age populations of Mexico, Central America, and the Caribbean Basin is likely to produce a continual flow of illegal immigrants.

Every year, the President, through the Coordinator of Refugees in the State Department, determines the number of refugees to be admitted during that particular year and the areas from which these refugees may be admitted. The ceiling fell from 231,000 in 1980 to 67,000 in 1986 but then rose again to 125,000 in 1990. There are currently between 13 and 15 million refugees worldwide. Unlike other entrants, refugees are entitled to special training programs designed to facilitate their adjustment to the United States and to expedite their transition to self-sufficiency.

Substantial changes have been occurring in both the size and the composition of legal immigration. First, the number of immigrants has been rising sharply. In 1965, slightly fewer than 300,000 permanent immigrants were admitted to the United States. During the 1970s, that number averaged about 440,000 annually; and during the late 1980s, it averaged over 600,000 per year. Second, the origin of immigrants has shifted dramatically; the share coming from Europe has fallen while the proportions from Asia and Latin America have risen. The overall number of immigrants has grown in part because of the increased number of families being reunited. Moreover, the number of temporary business workers, intrabusiness transfers, and students increased dramatically in the 1980s in contrast with the fairly stable number of legal immigrants admitted annually.

The United States has been filling some of its labor needs explicitly through the import of temporary labor. In 1987, more than 600,000 temporary workers were admitted to the country, compared with fewer than 54,000 as lawful permanent residents under the occupational preference categories of current law; this is a ratio of more than 10 to 1.

Congressional proposals to increase legal immigration and the number of independent legal immigrants admitted under labor market criteria, combined with IRCA's agricultural labor provisions, signal a move toward a more economically oriented immigration policy in the next decade.

ECONOMIC CONSIDERATIONS

Regardless of whether immigrants are admitted for humanitarian or economic reasons, most wind up in the labor force. For this reason alone, we should explicitly consider labor market issues in setting immigration policy.

A major concern is whether immigrants create jobs or take them away from the indigenous population. Many analysts argue that immigration benefits the U.S. economy and does not hurt the economic interests of those already here. As *The Economic Report of the President, 1986* noted, "The net effect of an increase in labor supply due to immigration is to increase the aggregate income of the native-born population."[1] Existing evidence suggests no or a very small displacement effect on native-born American workers. The evidence, however, does suggest disproportionate wage effects on prior cohorts of immigrants and on low-skill workers. Other evidence suggests disproportionate effects on all workers in areas where there is a high concentration of immigrants.[2]

Short-term labor displacement due to immigration appears to be highest in the highly competitive sectors, some low-skill occupations (e.g., janitors), labor market areas with high proportions of immigrants, and foreign-labor-intensive sectors. In general, the distributional effects are the strongest where the industrial structures of local areas are susceptible to displacement and the flow of immigrants is higher and more sustained.

The issue of displacement is far from fully settled. Indeed, the generally favorable evaluation of immigration by economists is in sharp contrast with popular opinion in some quarters, which emphasizes the job-displacement effects. This discrepancy can be explained in part by the fact that studies finding little or no displacement and little effect on wages are generally based on economy-wide long-term aggregate analyses, which usually pass over the question of short-run displacement and differential impacts among areas and industries. In contrast, public opinion often focuses on short-term displacement and lower wages in particular industries and regions, largely ignoring the possibility of long- term job creation.

The growing tightness in the supply of labor offers an unprecedented opportunity to address a broad range of chronic social problems through the singular channel of productive and rewarding employment. Recourse to immigration should not be permitted to substitute for bringing hard-to-employ workers into the work force and helping them become self-sufficient. We need to recognize the social, as well as economic, value of bringing disadvantaged people into the work force and to weigh this benefit against the economic potential of still higher rates of immigration.

The way to avoid conflicts between seeking to expand employment among the disadvantaged and immigration is to educate opinion leaders and the public about the real impact of immigration, reinforce efforts to bring the disadvantaged into the work force, and direct immigration policy toward eligibility for workers who will fill job shortages for which there is limited competition with indigenous Americans.

Based on these considerations, we believe several economic considerations should guide the design of U.S. immigration policy.

- **Increasing the aggregate number of immigrants and the proportion admitted specifically to enter the labor market could have a beneficial economic effect.**

- **Short-run displacement and/or earnings dampening effects are not always negligible and cannot be ignored, although they may be alleviated by appropriate sectoral and skill targeting.**

- **Better understanding of the effects of cumulative sustained waves of immigrants in specific areas and industries is needed in order to adjust policy to alleviate these problems.**

- **Giving preference to immigrants with skills in labor-short vocations, institutions, and regions would help minimize the displacement of native-born workers.**

- **Immigration should not be a substitute for bringing more disadvantaged citizens into the work force.**

These considerations suggest the advisability of increasing the proportion of immigrants admitted to enter the labor market in a manner that balances other policy goals. The current ratio of labor market to other immigrants is 1 to 10. (In Canada, that ratio has ranged from 1 to 2 in 1978 to 3 to 5 in 1987.) **We recommend that the ratio of permanent immigrants permitted entry under labor market classifications move gradually from the current 1 to 10 ratio to at least a 4 to 10 ratio by 1998.** The combination of increasing aggregate legal immigration and a gradual shift in the ratio toward labor market criteria should permit this change to occur without negative impact on other policy goals such as family reunification. Moreover, the spouses and children of labor market immigrants should continue to be permitted entry, thereby further serving the goal of keeping families together.

SOCIAL CONSIDERATIONS

Polls and other research indicate that over the past three decades, native residents have become more negative about illegal immigration in particular and about immigration in general. At the root of these attitudes, there is increasing concern over not only the economic effects of immigration but also the social and cultural effects. Historically, such concerns have accompanied every new wave of immigrants entering the country, but the current flow of immigrants differs from past groups in several ways.

The current wave of immigration is already the second longest in U.S. history, and it is expected to continue. (The longest was between 1880 and 1914, although it was interrupted by World War I.) Thus, any real or imagined adverse affects are continuously being reinforced by a steadily increasing stream of immigrants. Because the native population has a low birth rate, immigrants and their children account for a major proportion of current population growth (30 to 40 percent, depending on estimates of illegal immigration) and a growing proportion (20 percent or more) of new entrants to the labor force. There is now a predominance of Asian and Latin American immigrants, who may be regarded by those descended from European immigrants as more alien than European immigrants, although immigrants are now coming into a society where ethnic consciousness and diversity are not only accepted but increasingly encouraged. Significant segments of the country's population perceive continued population growth and urbanization as a threat to their quality of life, and immigration is viewed as a major source of this rapid growth. All these changes raise issues that bear on the other challenges to developing immigration policy.

Until recently, most research on the labor market experience of immigrants found that they eventually outperformed the native population. Some recent studies suggest that the latest waves of immigrants have not replicated the success of previous waves and offer several possible explanations for these alleged trends. One is that the markets for new immigrants and the native-born are increasingly segmented. There has been an increase in the concentration of immigrants in particular regions of the country. Their concentration and restricted geographic mobility may lower their relative wages. In addition, the skill profile of immigrants may have changed. Some immigrants may have fewer marketable skills than their predecessors. But it is also clear that an increasing number of new immigrants are starting their own businesses. Thus, the less industrious immigrants may be overrepresented in the analyses of wages while the self-employed and entrepreneurial immigrants achieve higher earnings that are not captured in these analyses. Another explanation may be that discrimination against the foreign-born has increased because Orientals and Latin Americans are visibly different from those of European descent.

These explanations are speculative and are mentioned primarily to indicate factors that must be considered in designing an effective, more economically oriented immigration policy. Clearly, the policy prescriptions, if any are needed, will differ significantly depending on whether the prevailing explanations for the trends recently identified are institutional (e.g., discrimination), structural (e.g., self-employment, market segmentation), or related to the skill levels of current immigrants.

FOREIGN POLICY ISSUES

If U.S. immigration policy were to shift in favor of labor market considerations, it might intensify two specific concerns among those countries from which the immigrants are coming: the brain drain and the effect on remittances.

Professionals and skilled workers are usually in short supply in developing countries, so there is concern that increasing the number of them admitted into the United States might lead to shortages in some occupations in their home countries. This might be seen as constricting economic performance, which, in turn could strain U.S. relations with these countries. These concerns might be further exacerbated by U.S. policies that reduced outmigration of those who have limited skill or who are unemployed.

For some countries, such as El Salvador, the Dominican Republic, and Mexico, remittances from immigrants to the United States to relatives they left behind represent a significant source of capital. In Mexico, official estimates of annual remittances are as high as $1 billion a year, making it the third to fourth main source of foreign exchange. Too little is known about the propensity to send remittances to predict how changes in the composition of immigration might affect remittances to specific countries, but it is clearly a significant concern for a number of countries.

In addition, increased immigration could constrain U.S. foreign policy options by creating domestic lobbies for policies affecting the immigrants' countries of origin.

We believe that these questions require more explicit attention than they have been given in the current U.S. immigration policy debate. U.S. immigration policy should be broadly conceived to improve economic performance and job growth in countries that generate emigration.

ADMINISTRATION OF IMMIGRATION POLICY

In the past, Congress has adjusted immigration policy only after long intervals. Given the current pace of change, responsiveness to the needs of the economy may require more frequent adjustments in the level and composition of immigration. At a minimum, we should expect that these needs are likely to differ in periods of high unemployment and low unemployment. This would be especially vital to minimize any possibility of displacing native labor. Moreover, a variety of federal agencies are currently involved in making and implementing immigration policy, and they must deal with a broad range of objectives, criteria, and reviews of individual applicants. A much more coordinated policy system is needed. **We recommend that U.S. immigration law establish a framework and a broad set of goals that leave adequate flexibility for rapid adjustments to changing labor markets.**

The vast number of illegal immigrants have undermined efforts to develop a coherent immigration policy while engendering disrespect for the nation's laws and dangerous conditions for those here illegally. **If U.S. immigration policy is to be effective and credible, it is clearly essential that enforcement be strict, swift, and certain.**

The Immigration and Naturalization Service (INS) has been underfunded, and the problem is getting worse. The administration, in its budget request for fiscal 1990, asked for only $370 million in refugee-assistance funds, almost 20 percent less than the $461 million allotted last year. At the same time, the administration has proposed accepting 125,000 refugees in fiscal 1990, up from 106,000 last year. Underfunding is limiting not only the agency's operating capability but also its ability to collect the information it needs to monitor the implementation of policy and assess its effects.

Effective policy making, implementation (especially enforcement), and evaluation of U.S. immigration demand adequate resources; we recommend realistic funding for the Immigration and Naturalization Service that projects increases over the next five years commensurate with the agency's growing responsibilities.

The absence of good information makes policy design and evaluation problematic. There is little data collected on the arrival and characteristics of both permanent and temporary immigrants, and there is no analysis of their labor force experience. Thus, we cannot assess incremental changes in legal immigration policy in the broader context of U.S. immigration policy.

The IRCA mandated that the President issue a comprehensive immigration-impact report to Congress every three years. But that analysis may not be enough to create flexible and effective policies.

Because immigration is going to play a major role in defining labor supply and demand for the foreseeable future, we believe that the formulation and coordination of immigration policy should be elevated to a higher, more visible level within the Executive Branch and that it be tied more specifically to work force and economic policy.

Chapter 8

The Labor Force Potential of Older Workers

An array of current policies and practices fosters an all-or-nothing view of work as people get older: their choice is generally to continue working full- time all year or go into full retirement. Individuals may find themselves pushed from too much work to too much leisure, with no intermediate steps. Many older people would welcome a wider range of alternatives, and from the standpoint of the nation's economy, the shrinking pool of new entrants to the U.S. labor force from the post-baby-boom generation could be augmented if we change our attitudes toward utilizing older workers.

Retirement policies need more *flexibility* instead of the current rigidity. For some workers, early retirement is a welcome respite; for others, full-time work until age 70 or beyond may be desirable. For still others, some continuing employment would be welcomed if they could reduce the pace or pressure of work or develop more flexible hours.

We believe that it is possible to help older workers stay active on the job longer in ways that will be beneficial for them and for the U.S. economy. Longer working lives will have a high payoff in the changing demographic environment, translating into more workers, more taxpayers, and fewer dependents.

Today's retirement policies were developed during the Great Depression when the primary concern was to create jobs for the young and to guarantee the old and infirm a decent reward for their years at work. These policies were based on a life expectancy of about 60 years, compared with today's average life span of 75 years. Increasing longevity combined with longer periods of schooling and earlier retirement means a growing number of Americans will spend as many years in nonwork activity as they have spent in the labor force.

The dramatic increase in the number of retirees in the United States and in the typical length of their retirement pose challenges for the labor market as well as for our retirement income and health-care financing systems. If we can find new ways to keep more older workers active, even while recognizing that some will want to retire earlier, we can relieve the pressure on younger workers and keep our public and private pension programs viable.

CHANGES IN THE LABOR FORCE PARTICIPATION OF OLDER WORKERS

The U.S. Department of Labor projects that more than 14 million people 60 to 69 years old will be out of the labor force by the year 2000, resulting in a net loss of more than 1 million potential workers aged 60 and over during the next decade. Labor force participation rates among the elderly have declined steadily since the 1930s, when half of all men over 65 and 13 percent of women over 55 were participating in the paid labor force. Today fewer than 15 percent of males and 8 percent of females over age 65 are working, even on a part-time basis.

During this same period, life expectancy at age 65 increased from 12 to 14.2 years for males and from 13.6 to 18.7 years for females. As a result, not only is the population of older Americans considerably larger than it was a generation or two ago, but an increasing proportion of this group is living to be much older.

The falling labor force participation rates of older Americans are really part of a broader trend among males of all ages that has been emerging since 1970. For males ages 25 to 44, the participation rate declined from 96 percent to 95 percent between 1970 and 1985. Although this appears to be a small decline, it represents almost 370,000 individuals who are not in the labor force at prime age. For the group ages 45 to 54, the rate declined from 94.3 percent to 91 percent over the same period, a loss of another 362,000 workers. The decline in labor force participation among 55- to 64-year-old males has been much larger, from 88.7 percent in 1954 to 67.2 percent in 1989. Moreover, a substantially smaller proportion of retirees under 65 cite illness or disability as the reason for not working in the 1980s than was the case in the 1950s. This suggests that early retirement is not being driven by deteriorating health.

Mandatory retirement has been postponed to age 70 in most industries, but such provisions affect less than half the work force. Moreover, fewer than 5 percent of employees in jobs with a mandatory retirement age work up until that age. The net result is that no more than 2 percent of all workers appear directly affected by such provisions.

Early retirement was encouraged by many firms in the 1970s and early 1980s as they reduced their labor forces or substituted younger entry-level workers for older, more highly paid employees. In 1986, for example, a quarter of the companies surveyed by Charles P. Spencer & Associates offered employees incentives to retire early. Although corporate downsizing has affected all age groups, older workers have been the special targets of many such efforts, often through incentives for early retirement. Many workers were also discharged as plants closed, and there were substantially fewer opportunities for new employment if they were past their mid-forties.

THE ROLE OF SOCIAL SECURITY AND PENSIONS

The combined effect of the income floor provided by Social Security benefits and the loss of these benefits if earned income exceeded a threshold level offered powerful incentives to older workers to leave the labor force during the 1940s. In the 1950s, private pension coverage began to spread, providing additional incentives to retire by age 65, if not earlier. In the 1970s, rapid increases in the real value of Social Security benefits further contributed to the attractiveness of retirement.

Social Security benefit levels have tripled in real terms since 1945. The ratio of monthly benefits to preretirement earnings of the average worker retiring at age 65 increased from 19 percent in 1950 to 51 percent in 1980, with the biggest boost occurring between 1969 and 1974. At the same time, combined marginal tax rates (federal, state, and Social Security) increased the penalty for continued labor force participation, particularly when combined with the Social Security earnings test. Although there have been dramatic cuts in federal income tax rates in the past decade, the reverse is true for state income taxes and Social Security payroll taxes, particularly at lower levels of income.

Current Social Security rules create strong financial incentives to remain in the labor force until at least age 62, coupled with disincentives to continue working after age 65. In 1990, earnings over $9,340 per year are effectively taxed at a marginal rate of 33 percent; there is a loss of one dollar of Social Security benefits for each three dollars earned above that level.

Congress has considered raising the ceiling or even eliminating it. Only 9 percent of older Americans actually lose benefits because of earnings from work, but the potential labor lost as a result is difficult to estimate. In any event, current policy still sends a negative message regarding work for Americans 65 years of age and over; income from investments does not count against Social Security benefits, but earnings from wages and salaries reduce benefits.

Government policy has become more neutral toward early retirement in recent years, and a number of encouraging developments can be noted. The federal government outlawed mandatory retirement for most workers in 1985. In 1986, Congress required employers to credit years of service worked after age 65 toward future Social Security benefits. In the 1983 Social Security Amendments, Congress stipulated that the normal retirement age will climb one month per year beginning in 2003, reaching age 67 in 2027. The benefit reduction associated with early retirement will also be increased in stages from 20 percent (its current level) in 2003 to 30 percent in 2027. In addition, the benefit increase provided to those who postpone receiving Social Security benefits until after normal retirement age will increase from 3 percent a year to 8 percent.[1] Of course, the timetable for the increase in the normal retirement age under Social Security could be accelerated; it is not necessary to wait until the early part of the next century. But the attractive way this was handled in 1983 is that today's older workers did not have their retirement planning disrupted while the next generation of retirees was given ample advance notice of a higher age for receiving full benefits.

Although the lower benefits associated with early retirement can be described as a disincentive to an early departure from the work force, the reality is more complex. Depending on a worker's own estimate of his or her life expectancy, the "lower but longer" benefit path may look quite attractive. In addition, real Social Security benefit levels have risen sharply since the 1960s, so workers can now get 80 percent of a much larger amount.

These other factors must be at work because the penalty for early retirement under Social Security is at least as strong now as it was thirty years ago, yet the proportion of workers opting for early retirement has soared. During the 1980s, 57.9 percent of males and 70.2 percent of females chose to begin payments at age 62; in 1961, only 4.7 percent of males and 37.4 percent of females had chosen this option.

Studies of beneficiaries actually show a substantial number of workers withdrawing from the labor force several years *before* age 62 when they are not eligible for *any* benefits. Depressed employment opportunities for older workers in the 1970s and 1980s may explain a great deal of the substantial shift in behavior since the 1960s.

Private pension income is important for a much smaller group of the population than is Social Security. Currently, only 30 percent of retirees receive private pension payments, and such payments account for only 15 percent of the income of the aged. But nearly half of all workers now in the labor force have some sort of pension coverage. As a result, we can expect a much larger proportion of future retirees to receive such payments, which will make up a growing share of older Americans' incomes. When these payments are combined with Social Security income, private pension recipients appear able to replace well over half of their after-tax preretirement earnings. Federal civilian and military retirement programs encourage retirement at 55 (earlier in the case of some military personnel). Additional early-retirement programs in the private sector have added to this trend since the 1970s. Although Social Security should provide an opposing incentive, some private plans have allowed early retirees to receive a supplemental payment to make up for Social Security income until it kicks in. One survey found that 62 was the most common retirement age, followed by 65.[2]

The majority of private pension plans provide strong incentives to stay in the labor force until a certain age (typically between 55 and 65) but decreasing returns for continued work thereafter. A recent study based on U.S. Bureau of Labor Statistics pension surveys found "substantial incentives to terminate work at the current job after the age of early retirement and even greater incentives to leave after the age of normal retirement."[3] The study found considerable variation in retirement ages and in work incentives among industries and firms. In the transportation sector, for example, almost 62 percent of plans provide for retirement at age 55. In these firms, workers would experience a 27 percent reduction in effective annual compensation by continuing to work at age 56. In manufacturing, only 6 percent of plans offer retirement at age 55, with two-thirds reaching normal retirement at age 65. And if the worker were to continue after age 65, the decline in pension accrual results in an effective reduction in compensation of about 21 percent.

In recent years, many private pension plans have lowered the age at which retired workers may receive unreduced normal benefits. In 1988, nearly 60 percent of the participants in defined-benefit pension plans could retire before the age of 65 with full benefits. The most common minimum age for early retirement is 55, and almost all participants can retire with reduced benefits by age 60. Moreover, fewer than one-fifth of pension plan participants now face a full actuarial reduction in annuities.[4]

Given the declining rates of benefit accrual after early retirement and the negative rates after normal retirement, it is not surprising that many workers choose retirement before it is mandatory. Indeed, employers may design plans to offer these incentives in the belief that older workers become less productive even as their wages remain high. If firms are to change their pension plans to encourage longer working lives, they also may need to upgrade workers' skills more often to enhance their productivity.

LABOR MARKET INCENTIVES FOR THE POTENTIAL RETIREE

The retirement decisions of older workers during the past two decades appear to have been influenced both by the "pull" of nonlabor income provided through Social Security and private pensions and the "push" of labor market conditions. Although the ownership of assets by older Americans as a group is high, income from assets is not an important part of total income for two-thirds of today's elderly. Pensions, Social Security, and employment opportunities are the dominant factors in the decision for the majority of older workers today.

Labor market conditions in the 1970s and early 1980s were such that job opportunities for unemployed older workers were often nonexistent or highly unattractive. However, these conditions have already begun to change as smaller cohorts of youths have entered the labor force since 1983 and increases in the labor force participation rate of women have slowed. Real wages, at least for those with a college education, are expected to continue increasing into the 1990s and beyond. On the surface, these changing labor market conditions would seem to portend an increase in labor force activity by older workers. Since the real attrition among older males has been among the less educated, however, the problem may not be cured by a tighter labor market alone.

Workers who are less educated and who hold blue-collar jobs are also likely to have more health problems. As they grow older, the pull away from the labor force is stronger because work becomes more difficult physically and leisure more attractive, even at a lower income. Although health has improved, on average, coverage and payments under disability programs have also increased over the past two decades. Time not spent at work can also be used for activities that create value for the individual, such as caring for an ailing relative, remodeling a home, or volunteering in the community. The opportunity cost of these activities is lower when wages are relatively low, which is consistent with the concentration of the decline in labor force participation among blue-collar men.

Work at its best has noneconomic values that the retiree gives up: prestige, social ties, and mental challenges. But early retirees from the labor force appear to be those less likely to find these benefits in their work and thus more willing to substitute other activities. In addition, many pension plans provide a negative return to additional work beyond the minimum retirement age. Thus, it is understandable that as the health and stamina of some older workers decline and the choice they face is between full-time work and total retirement, they will choose total retirement.

In the face of a declining labor supply we need to reexamine our attitudes toward part-time work; this is true for older workers as well as for parents with child-care responsibilities, students, and others. If workers in their mid-fifties to mid-sixties could choose to remain active with either shorter workweeks or increased leave time, many more might choose to continue working. Access to group medical benefits and additional accruing of pension benefits are likely to make part-time work more attractive to potential retirees, particularly if early-retirement incentives are changed to encourage such behavior.

IS THERE A DEMAND FOR OLDER WORKERS?

The evidence of the past decade indicates that significant declines in labor force participation are occurring among males who are not eligible for pension or disability income and who are too young to collect even reduced Social Security benefits. The primary cause of withdrawal in these cases appears to be declining demand for their labor.

The unit labor cost of the older worker is often higher than that of a younger worker, even when their wages are equal. For example, if a firm provides medical benefits, the costs are often experience-rated; the more older workers on the payroll, the higher those costs will be. Since 1986, business has been the primary payer of medical costs even for workers old enough for Medicare coverage. The existence of a pension plan may also raise the unit labor cost of the older worker relative to that of the younger.

During the past two decades, the abundance of young workers with relatively low entry-level wages made them much more attractive than older workers with higher wage expectations, and rising employee benefit costs increased the cost differential between these groups. It is not surprising, therefore, that many firms have shown a bias in favor of young workers. Moreover, rapid technological change also gave recently trained workers a competitive edge over those who had been in the labor force longer. Years of experience sometimes seemed to translate into lower rather than higher productivity.

However, the emerging shortage of young workers and the increasing deficits in the skills and knowledge of this smaller cohort will improve employment opportunities for older workers in the 1990s. Consequently, we can expect more of them to remain in the labor force – if not in the same job, then in another position.

Firms need to plan for the future by restructuring the retirement incentives in their pension plans and by taking steps to ensure that workers who are retained will maintain high levels of productivity. Education and on-the-job training can no longer be confined to new entrants into the labor force but must be a regular part of everyone's working life.

Utilization of older workers may require rethinking the ways in which jobs are designed and the flexibility of policies regarding voluntary leave. Employers may want to develop more opportunities for older workers to scale down hours or responsibilities and should also consider new ways to attract those retired from full-time jobs back into the work force on a part-time or temporary basis.

BUSINESS INITIATIVES TO UTILIZE OLDER WORKERS

The realization is growing that retirees constitute a pool of trained talent to be tapped, but so far only a few companies have done so. One of the first and best-known examples is The Travelers Companies, which polled its workers ages 55 and over in 1980 and discovered that 22 percent of them planned to work past age 65 in their current jobs; most of those responding said they would prefer part-time work at the company. Having initiated an Older Americans Program a year earlier, Travelers then moved to establish its retiree job bank (see page 148).

Another company that has instituted an innovative policy to keep older skilled workers on the job is Teledyne Wisconsin Motor, a manufacturer of heavy-duty engines. Teledyne conducted an age audit in 1977 and discovered that it had more potential early retirees than workers. Concerned about both a squeeze on its pension fund and a shortage of skilled people, the company created its Golden Bridge program (see page 149).

Xerox tries to keep productive older workers from retiring early by giving them job options. Unionized hourly employees who meet certain age and tenure requirements can bid on jobs that make fewer physical demands or are less stressful. These jobs are generally lower paying as well, and the reduction in pay is split between Xerox and the employee. Since this job-mobility program was established in 1980, more than 10 percent of eligible employees have chosen to take advantage of it.

The Aerospace Corporation values older workers highly for their skills and experience. Half its current work force will retire within the next decade, and Aerospace has 145 full-time regular employees who are 65 or older; their jobs range from scientists and engineers to office and shop workers. The company values continuity on long-term projects; it also

---

OLDER AMERICANS PROGRAM AT THE TRAVELERS COMPANIES

The Travelers Older Americans Program, initiated by the company's chief executive officer in 1979, has as its primary goal increasing the economic security of older people through extended employment. The Travelers Retiree Job Bank offers part-time employment to retirees. The company estimates that its Job Bank saves the company $1.5 million per year in temporary agency fees while meeting the need for experienced and reliable temporary workers.

Travelers abolished mandatory retirement in 1980 (six years before similar national legislation) and altered its pension plan to allow retirees to work up to 960 hours per year without jeopardizing their retirement benefits. The Job Bank was opened to Travelers' retirees living in the Hartford, Connecticut, area in 1981. In 1985, the company began recruiting retirees from other area companies through an effort dubbed the "Unretirement Campaign." The original effort was broadened this way because the demand for older workers by supervisors had grown beyond the supply generated by Travelers' own retirees.

The Job Bank matches retirees' skills and schedules with temporary job openings. Retirees fill in during absences and delays in hiring full-time personnel and for special projects. The Job Bank is able to accommodate their personal schedules through flexible hours and to help them keep their skills current with business needs through computer training opportunities.

Retirees participating in the Older Americans Program are paid the midpoint of the salary grade for each job they fill. Approximately 750 retirees are registered in the Job Bank, about half of them former Travelers employees. During a typical week, about 250 of them are working at the company. Many perform clerical and secretarial work; others coordinate special events, conduct research, and work as underwriters. The Job Bank satisfies about 60 percent of the company's requirements for temporary help.

rehires retirees as "casual" employees, typically to continue working on the same tasks. These employees can work up to 1,000 hours annually and still receive pension benefits under a revision to the company's pension plan. Aerospace added a Retiree Technical and Administrative Pool in 1987 (see page 150).

Western Savings and Loan Association in Phoenix decided to hire retirees for full-time jobs having to deal with the public. Western saw this as a way to attract new customers from the growing population of retirees in Arizona. These new employees hold positions ranging from tellers to branch managers. This is a strategy that other companies located in areas with large concentrations of retirees may want to consider.

Whereas companies such as Travelers and Aerospace maintain their own internal pools of temporary workers recruited from the ranks of retirees, others rely on outside temporary agencies to supply their needs. Kelly Services is one of the nation's oldest and largest providers of temporary help, hiring more than half a million people annually to work in nearly all sectors of the economy. Since 1987, Kelly has been making a special

---

GOLDEN BRIDGE PROGRAM AT TELEDYNE WISCONSIN MOTOR

Fearing a potentially large loss of skilled workers through early retirement, Milwaukee's Teledyne Wisconsin Motor created its Golden Bridge program as a transition from work to retirement. It features added vacation time, increased life insurance, higher pension benefits, and improved benefits for surviving spouses.

Factory employees age 58 to 62 who have thirty years of service are entitled to twenty extra days of vacation annually, and those over 62 get twenty-five extra days. This time can either be taken as paid leave or as a cash-out payable at the end of the year or when they retire.

Older employees also get an additional $1,000 of life insurance and a one-third increase in pension benefits for each year of participation. In addition, surviving spouses of employees who work to age 65 get 60 percent (instead of 55) of basic pension benefits.

About fifty employees are participating in the program at any given time, with ten to twelve new people joining it each year. The majority of participants work in the factory. Salaried employees must be 60 years old (instead of 58) to join.

effort to recruit older temporary workers through its ENCORE program (see page 151).

In addition, several recently formed temporary service agencies confine their recruiting efforts to older workers. Superior Senior Services was begun in 1987 in Minneapolis and has an enrollment of more than 300 older job seekers. Retiree Skills, Inc., serves 300 businesses in Tucson with more than 700 retirees and plans to set up franchises in other parts of Arizona and perhaps eventually in other western states. Interim Management Company in New York and The Corporate Staff in San Francisco specialize even further by providing temporary employment for senior executives who have chosen early retirement or had it chosen for them as the result of corporate reorganizations.

Intertek Services is a California company that supplies quality-control engineers and technicians from a roster of 5,000 retired and semiretired recruits, some in their seventies. Recruitment is done through professional journals as well as by word of mouth; Intertek then screens

TECHNICAL AND ADMINISTRATIVE POOL AT AEROSPACE CORPORATION

Aerospace Corporation of El Segundo, California had a long-established policy of rehiring its retirees, usually bringing them back as consultants to work on specific projects. When the Internal Revenue Service began scrutinizing independent contractor arrangements with a single employer, Aerospace revised its pension plan in 1982 to allow those receiving benefits to work up to 1,000 hours a year without losing them.

Then, in 1987, the company began operating a new skills bank, making an inventory of the skills available among retirees who were interested in returning to work. This bank is actually an internal pool of retirees available for temporary job assignments and is called the Retiree Technical and Administrative Pool. The pool focused on engineering and technical skills from the outset, although retired secretaries and other administrative support staff are included as well.

The original nucleus of the pool was 75 retirees, mostly engineers and technicians, who already had part-time working arrangements with the company. The pool now numbers about 250 retirees out of a total of 1,000.

candidates and checks their credentials. Those selected work as independent contractors and are free to decline assignments. More such firms can be expected to appear as the population of retired engineers and technicians grows while the American education system continues to produce limited numbers of graduates in technical fields.

Two companies that openly favor older workers because of their superior performance are Texas Refinery Corporation (TRC) and F.W. Dodge Company. TRC has an age-neutral recruiting policy, but its president considers older workers better motivated, more loyal and reliable, and harder working than many younger ones. About 500 out of a 3,000-member sales force are in their sixties, seventies, and even eighties, and this over-60 age group contains a number of the company's leading salespeople. They work as independent contractors, mostly part-time to supplement Social Security benefits.

F.W. Dodge Company is a data-gathering firm with employees located throughout the country. It now hires retirees on a *permanent* part-time basis, instead of the temporary part-timers it used to employ; this is a little costlier, but these older employees have proven more reliable while producing higher-quality work. In response to the company's original recruitment effort, 90 percent of the available positions in 120 cities were

---

ENCORE PROGRAM AT KELLY SERVICES

Kelly Services' ENCORE program is a special recruiting effort to attract people aged 55 and over into its work force of temporary employees. All 700 Kelly branch offices in the U.S. and Canada are involved in this outreach effort.

Kelly has found that older workers and retirees often prefer the flexibility of part-time, short-lived assignments. Many employees in the company's technical division are retirees returning to work temporarily for the companies from which they retired. Temporary work also provides a good way for older people to re-enter the job market after being away from it.

Kelly estimates that about 10 percent of its 550,000 current temps are older than 55. An Older Worker Committee has now been formed at the National Association of Temporary Service Agencies (NATS) as well, to stimulate recruiting and education efforts. Local committees are surveying employment initiatives for older workers through NATS chapters around the country.

filled by retirees in their sixties. These employees work anywhere from three or four days a month to four or five days a week.

The terms of some defined-benefit pension plans make it necessary to employ retirees either as independent contractors or through outside temporary help agencies. Some companies that had such restrictive clauses have rewritten their plans to allow part-time employment up to the 1,000-hour limit beyond which part-time employees must be eligible to earn service credits in any ERISA-qualified pension plan. Companies with defined-benefit pension plans that are considering establishing their own internal temporary pools (as Travelers has done) need to examine the specific terms of those plans.

RETIREE HEALTH CARE BENEFITS

More than a fifth of older Americans receive company-paid health insurance benefits after retiring. These benefits typically are the same as those provided to active workers; retiree health insurance plans become the second payer after Medicare for retirees who are 65 or older and not working. Many retiree health benefit plans are in trouble because, unlike pension plans, they are not funded. The Financial Accounting Standards Board is expected soon to issue a directive requiring companies to show these unfunded liabilities on their balance sheets; the Employee Benefit Research Institute estimated the total liability for private employers in 1988 at nearly $250 billion, about $100 billion for current retirees and another $150 billion for current workers.

Economic, demographic, and political factors are converging to heighten concern about the future viability of retiree health benefits. Health care costs continue to rise much faster than the general price level, the population will be aging more rapidly in the future, and the trend toward early retirement has left many companies paying benefits to more people who are not yet eligible for Medicare. The federal government has shifted much of the cost of health care for active workers ages 65 or older to private employers by making them the primary payer instead of Medicare; this change in public policy merely increases the disincentive to retain employees past age 65.

All this portends a crisis in retiree health benefits that can be headed off only by restructuring and better managing health care for the elderly in order to bring its cost under control. The coordination of retiree benefits with Medicare and private Medigap policies purchased by many older Americans is part of such a strategy.

For example, Southern California Edison and the Amalgamated Life Insurance Company are exploring the possibilities of serving as joint administrators of both Medicare and Edison-funded retiree health benefits. Under this proposed arrangement, Medicare would pay the companies 95 percent of what it would otherwise spend for the retirees. The companies would combine these resources with their own and provide combined Medicare and Edison-sponsored coverage.

Although it is important to better coordinate benefits among Medicare, private Medigap policies, and employer-sponsored retiree health insurance, meeting the health-care needs of a growing elderly population will require more than improving insurance management. The real problem is not so much *coordinating* existing insurance, which primarily covers acute medical care, as it is *developing* insurance for long-term care.

Private long-term care insurance is growing rapidly, and over 100 companies now sell it. Policies have been redesigned to meet consumer needs, and the National Association of Insurance Commissioners has developed a model plan. Employers can play an important role in making such insurance available to their workers, and the federal government could invigorate this market by making the federal tax status of contributions to long-term-care insurance comparable to that of current health insurance contributions. Government can also play a role by reshaping its entitlement programs to reflect the growing importance of long-term care.

In addition to improving the financing system for long-term care, we need to improve the delivery system to enhance the quality of life of very old people. Demographic statistics make it clear that the quantity of life is increasing, but this creates a challenge to assure a decent quality of life as well. This will require the development of new financial incentives and social services that help people remain at home as long as possible. It will also require the country to face difficult choices about how much health care is enough.

POLICY RECOMMENDATIONS

Private pension plans and Social Security have built-in economic incentives that favor retirement. Labor force withdrawal appears to be particularly encouraged by private pension plans that give workers negative returns for staying on the job as early as age 56 in some industries. If modifications to pension plans, health benefit programs, and the structure of working arrangements can be made to encourage many older workers to stay in the labor force just a few years longer, it would help substantially to meet future labor market requirements imposed by demographic changes. It would also help the long-run viability of the Social Security and Medicare programs.

If the financial incentives for retirement are altered, attitudes toward retirement are likely to change as well, particularly as individuals perceive the long and active life that they may well lead after age 65. This would bode well for the labor force of the twenty-first century.

CED recommends the following changes in public and private policies to recruit more older Americans to help in meeting the goal of an adequate and productive work force in the coming decades:

1. **Remove the earned-income test for Social Security payments after age 65.** This proposal can be made "revenue-neutral" through taxation of a larger share of Social Security benefits as recipients' incomes increase.

2. **Restructure pension plans that discourage work by older employees to make these plans neutral with respect to the incentive to continue working.**

3. **Move toward flexible hours in the workplace,** through benefit packages that allow workers to buy additional weeks of vacation or personal leave at attractive rates and through jobs built around reduced hours of work per week without the lower status and pay rates of traditional part-time jobs.

4. **Identify workers already retired who might be given incentives to re-enter the work force on a limited basis.**

5. **Invest in programs that maintain the productivity of older workers** by helping them accommodate to new technologies, or shift them to jobs that are less physically demanding or stressful. Much of this investment can take place in the private sector. But government can play a role as well, through adequate funding and stronger program designs in the JTPA, the Senior Community Service Employment Program, the Carl Perkins Vocational Education Act, and Adult Basic Education.

6. **Allow companies more flexibility in moving dollars from overfunded pension plans to underfunded retiree health benefit plans.**

7. **Actively pursue experiments in which the federal government and companies or unions jointly manage Medicare benefits and retiree health benefits.**

8. **Place greater emphasis in health benefit plans on preventing disability and helping disabled workers return to work.**

9. **Promote long-term care insurance, as well as greater voluntary activities to assist the frail elderly.***

*   *   *

The recommendations in this report are far ranging. They extend from efforts to assist the youngest of our citizens to post-retirement programs for the elderly. Together, they form a comprehensive blueprint for a competitive American work force.

Our hope is that this report will change the way the nation thinks about its human resources. Through the collective efforts of business, labor, and government, the United States can build a coherent strategy for unleashing the productive energies of its workforce in the years ahead.

---

*See memoranda by ELMER B. STAATS (page 163).

Appendix A

HIGHLIGHTS OF PROGRAM EFFECTS

	BENEFITS FOR CHILDREN	COST BENEFIT	PARTICIPATION
WIC – SPECIAL SUPPLEMENTAL FOOD PROGRAM FOR WOMEN, INFANTS AND CHILDREN	Reduction in infant mortality and births of low birthweight infants; reduced prevalence of anemia; improved cognitive skills	$1 investment in prenatal component of WIC has saved as much as $3 in short-term hospital costs	3.46 million participants – about 44% of those eligible – received WIC services in March 1987, up by 300,000 since Spring 1985.
PRENATAL CARE	Reduction in prematurity, low birthweight births and infant mortality; elimination or reduction of diseases and disorders during pregnancy	$1 investment can save $3.38 in cost of care for low birthweight infants	24% of live births in 1985 were to mothers who did not begin prenatal care in the first trimester of pregnancy. The rate for white births was 21%, for black births 38%. Figures reflect essentially no change since 1982.
MEDICAID	Decreased neonatal and infant mortality, and fewer abnormalities among children receiving EPSDT services	$1 spent on comprehensive prenatal care added to services for Medicaid recipients has saved $2 in infant's first year; lower health care costs for children receiving EPSDT services	In FY 1986, an estimated 9.95 million dependent children under 21 were served by Medicaid, including 2.14 million screened under EPSDT. Figures reflect an increase of 400,000 served under Medicaid, but a drop of half million screened under EPSDT in FY 1983. In calendar year 1986 there were 12.95 million children in families below the poverty line, compared to 14.3 in FY 1983.
CHILDHOOD IMMUNIZATION	Dramatic declines in incidence of rubella, mumps, measles, polio, diphtheria, tetanus and pertussis	$1 spent on Childhood Immunization Program saves $10 in later medical costs	In 1985, the total percent of children ages 1- 4 immunized against the major childhood diseases ranged from 73.8 for rubella to 87.0 for diphtheria-tetanus-pertussis. For those 5- 14, percent immunized ranged from 85.3 for rubella to 93 for DTP. Smaller proportions of children in both age groups were immunized against polio, measles and rubella in 1985 than in 1983.

PRESCHOOL EDUCATION	Increased school success, employability, and self esteem; reduced dependence on public assistance	$1 investment in quality preschool education returns $6 because of lower costs of special education, public assistance, and crime	In 1985, there were 10.7 million children ages 3-5. 5.9 million of them were enrolled in public and non-public pre-primary programs. 453,000 children – fewer than 1 out of every 5 eligible – were participating in Head Start as of September 1987. Since 1983, the number of children ages 3-5 and the number enrolled in public and non-public pre-primary programs increased by 500,000; Head Start participation is up by only 11,000.
COMPENSATORY EDUCATION	Achievement gains and maintenance of gains in reading and mathematics	Investment of $750 for year of compensatory education can save $3700 cost of repeating grade	In 1985, 4.9 million children – an estimated 50% of those in need – received Chapter I services under the LEA Basic Grant Program. This reflects an increase of 200,000 children since 1982-1983.
EDUCATION FOR ALL HANDICAPPED CHILDREN	Increased number of students receiving services in regular school setting; greater academic and employment success	Early educational intervention has saved school districts $1560 per disabled pupil	During School Year 1985-86, 4,121,104 children ages 3-21 were served under the State Grant program, up by approximately 27,000 children in 1983-84. The prevalence of handicaps in the population under age 21 is estimated to be 11.4% (9.5-10 million children).
YOUTH EMPLOYMENT AND TRAINING	Gains in employability, wages, and success while in school and afterwards	Job Corps returned $7,400 per participant, compared to $5,000in program costs (in 1977 dollars). FY 1982 service year costs for YETP $4,700; participants had annualized earnings gains of $1,810.	During Program Year July 1986-June 1987, 64,954 youths were enrolled in Job Corps, and 432,680 in JTPA Title IIA; 634,000 youths participated in summer youth programs. The annualized number of unemployed persons 16-21 years old in 1986 was 2,160,000. Numbers of youth participating in all activities decreased from the period October 1983 July 1984 to July 1986- June 1987, with the exception of participation in JTPA Title IIA.

158

ENDNOTES

CHAPTER 2

1. U.S. Department of Labor, *Monthly Labor Review,* November 1989, p. 5.

2. *Ibid.*

3. *Ibid.,* p. 5, 11.

4. *Ibid.,* p. 9.

5. R. Scott Fosler, ed., *Demographic Change and the American Future,* (Pittsburgh: University of Pittsburgh Press 1990).

6. U.S. Department of Labor, *Monthly Labor Review,* November 1989, p. 11.

7. *The Forgotten Half: Pathways to Success for America's Youth and Young Families,* (Washington, D.C.: Youth and America's Future: The William T. Grant Commission on Work, Family and Citizenship, 1988).

8. Sean Sullivan and Nancy S. Bagby, *Employer Initiatives in Disability Management and Rehabilitation* (Washington, D.C.: National Chamber Foundation, 1989), p. 1.

9. Gail E. Schwartz, et. al., *The Disability Management Source Book,* (Washington, D.C.: Washington Business Group on Health/Institute for Rehabilitation and Disability Management, 1989), p. 8.

10. *Investing in Our Children: Business and the Public Schools,* A Statement by the Research and Policy Committee of the Committee for Economic Development (New York: Committee for Economic Development, 1985), p. 2.

11. The Gallup Organization, *Geography: An International Gallup Survey, 1988,* conducted for the National Geographic Society, Princeton, New Jersey, 1988, p. 4.

12. The Gallup Organization, *Geography: An International Gallup Survey.*

13. U.S. Department of Labor, *op. cit.,* pp. 103, 105.

CHAPTER 3

1. See Ellen Galinsky, Dana E. Friedman, and the Families and Work Institute, "Education Before School: Investing in Quality Child Care," (paper prepared for the Committee for Economic Development, 1990). This report was produced as part of a CED project that is examining the child-care issue.

2. *U.S. Children and Their Families: Current Conditions and Recent Trends, 1989,* Report No. 101-356 of the Select Committee on Children, Youth, and Families, U.S. House of Representatives (Washington, D.C.: U.S. Government Printing Office, 1989).

3. P. Michael Timpane, "The Impact of Business Involvement on Education Reform," paper prepared for the Committee for Economic Development, 1990.

4. Adopted February 25, 1990 by the National Governors' Association at its Winter Meeting, "Consensus for Change: Setting National Goals for Excellence in Education & Environmental Quality," Washington, D.C., February 25-27, 1990.

5. John Chubb, "Why the Current Wave of School Reform Will Fail," *The Public Interest,* No. 90, Winter 1988, p. 42.

6. In 1989, at least twenty-nine states were funding some form of early- childhood programs, and several others were considering initiating programs.

7. Henry Levin, *The Educationally Disadvantaged: A National Crisis* (Philadelphia, PA: Public/Private Ventures, 1985), p. 8.

8. These issues are explored in The Business-Higher Education Forum, *American Potential: The Human Dimension*, (Washington, D.C.: Business- Higher Education Forum, 1988).

9. U.S. Department of Education, *Digest of Educational Statistics* (Washington, D.C.: U.S. Government Printing Office, 1986).

10. During the same period, college enrollment as a percentage of high school graduates increased from 32.7 to 33.7.

11. U.S. Department of Education, *Digest of Educational Statistics.*

12. *Trends in Student Aid 1980-1989,* The College Board, Washington, D.C.: August, 1989. Table 6.

13. Carnegie Foundation for the Advancement of Teaching and the American Council on Education, *Campus Life: In Search of Community,* (Princeton, N.J.: Princeton University Press, 1990)

CHAPTER 4

1. See R. Scott Fosler, *The Business Role in State Education Reform,* (New York: The Business Roundtable, 1990), and *The Business Roundtable Participation Guide: A Primer for Business on Education,* developed by the National Alliance for Business (New York: The Business Roundtable, 1990).

2. The members of the Business Coalition on Education Reform are the American Business Conference, Black Business Council, Business Roundtable, Committee for Economic Development, Conference Board, National Alliance of Business, National Association of Manufacturers, U.S. Chamber of Commerce, and U.S. Hispanic Chamber of Commerce. Affiliated organizations include the Council on Competitiveness and the Business-Higher Education Forum.

3. Marsha Levine and Roberta Trachtman, eds., *American Business and the Public School,* (New York: Teachers College Press, 1988).

4. Anthony P. Carnevale, Leila J. Gainer, and Ann S. Melzer, *Workplace Basics: The Skills Employers Want,* (Alexandria, VA: The American Society for Training and Development and the U.S. Department of Labor, 1989).

5. Paul Barton, *From School to Work,* Policy Information Report (Princeton, N.J.: Educational Testing Center, 1990), p. 11.

6. Commission on the Skills of the American Workforce, *America's Choice: High Skills or Low Wages!,* (Rochester, N.Y.: National Center on Education and the Economy, 1990).

7. Barton, p. 26.

8. The "Forgotten Half" described by the Commission on Work, Family and Citizenship. *The Forgotten Half: Pathways to Success for America's Youth and Young Families,* (Washington, D.C.: The William T. Grant Commission on Work, Family and Citizenship, 1988).

9. William Nothdurft, *SchoolWorks: Reinventing Public Schools to Create the Workforce of the Future,* (Washington, D.C.: The German Marshall Fund of the United States and The Brookings Institution, 1989). Several states, including Michigan and Indiana, have been adopting features of European training systems. The previously mentioned study by the National Center for Education and the Economy also suggests the features of various foreign systems that could be adapted to American training programs.

CHAPTER 5

1. Anthony P. Carnevale and Leila Gainer, *The Learning Enterprise*, (Washington, D.C.: American Society for Training and Development/U.S. Department of Labor, 1990).

2. Remarks of Jack E. Bowsher, Retired Director of Education External Programs, IBM Corporation, at CED Symposium on "The New America: Prospects for Population and Policy in the 21st Century," Washington, D.C., May 18, 1989.

3. Denis P. Doyle, "Developing Human Capital: The Role of the Private Sector," paper prepared for the Institute for Policy Studies, The Johns Hopkins University, Baltimore, Md., March 1989.

4. Anthony P. Carnevale, Leila J. Gainer and Ann S. Meltzer, *Workplace Basics: The Essential Skills Employers Want*, (San Francisco: Jossey-Bass, Inc., 1990).

5. Anthony P. Carnevale and Janet W. Johnston, *Training America: Strategies for the Nation*, (Alexandria, Va.: National Center on Education and the Economy/American Society for Training and Development, 1989).

6. See Ronald F. Ferguson and Helen F. Ladd, "Massachusetts," in R. Scott Fosler, ed., *The New Economic Role of American States* (New York: Oxford University Press, 1988), pp. 57-60.

7. Evelyn Ganzglass and Maria Heidcamp, *State Strategies To Train a Competitive Workforce: The Emerging Role of State-Funded Job Training Programs*, (Washington, D.C.: National Governors' Association, 1988).

8. Paul E. Barton, *A Better Fit between Unemployment Insurance and Retraining*, (Washington, D.C.: National Institute for Work and Learning, 1986).

9. Audrey Freedman, *The New Look in Wage Policy and Employee Relations*, (New York: The Conference Board, 1985).

10. Daniel Yankelovich, *Putting the Work Ethic to Work*, (New York: Public Agenda Foundation, 1983).

11. Employee Benefit Research Institute, "Pension Portability and What It Can Do for Retirement Income," Issue Brief No. 65, April 1987.

12. Employee Benefit Research Institute, "Pension Portability . . . ," op. cit.

CHAPTER 6

1. Edward D. Berkowitz and Monroe Berkowitz, "Incentives for Reducing the Costs of Disability," in Kenneth McLennan and Jack A. Meyer, eds., *Care & Cost: Current Issues in Health Policy*, (Boulder, Co.: Westview Press, 1989), pp. 203-226.

2. Dana E. Friedman, "The Impact of Child Care on the Bottom Line," prepared for the U.S. Department of Labor Commission on Workforce Quality and Labor Market Efficiency, Families and Work Institute, New York, 1989.

3. Dana E. Friedman, "Painting the Child Care Landscape, A Palette of Inadequacy and Innovation," in *Family and Work, Bridging the Gap*, Sylvia Ann Hewlett, et. al., eds., (Cambridge, Mass: Ballinger Publishing Company, 1986), pp. 67-89.

4. Friedman, "Painting the Child Care Landscape . . . ." op. cit.

5. Pat Choate and J. K. Linger, *The High-Flex Society*, (New York: Alfred A. Knopf, 1986).

6. Janice Castro, "Home Is Where the Heart Is," *Time*, October 3, 1988, pp. 46-53.

7. Friedman, "The Impact of Child Care on the Bottom Line," op. cit.

8. Friedman, "The Impact of Child Care on the Bottom Line," op. cit.

CHAPTER 7

1. *The Economic Report of the President, 1986* (Washington, D.C.: U.S. Government Printing Office, 1986), p. 222.

2. See George J. Borjas, *Friends or Strangers: The Impact of Immigrants on the U.S. Economy,* (New York: Basic Books, Inc., 1990), and Kevin F. McCarthy and R. Burciago Valdez, *Current and Future Effects of Mexican Immigration in California,* (Santa Monica, CA: The RAND Corporation, 1986).

CHAPTER 8

1. William J. Wiatrowski, "Supplementing Retirement until Social Security Begins," *Monthly Labor Review,* February 1990, p. 26.

2. Gary S. Fields and Olivia S. Mitchell, *Retirement, Pensions, and Social Security,* (Cambridge, MA: MIT Press, 1984).

3. Lawrence J. Kotlikoff and David A. Wise, "The Incentive Effects of Private Pension Plans," in Zvi Bodie, John B. Shoven and David A. Wise, eds., *Issues in Pension Economics,* (Chicago: University of Chicago Press, 1987).

4. Wiatrowski, op. cit.

162

Memoranda of Comment, Reservation, or Dissent

Page 13, THOMAS J. EYERMAN

The United States should use punishment to discourage illegal entry, but it should encourage many more skilled workers. We should not penalize people with skills coming to America due to our own inability to deal with the hard-to-employ situation. We need a sensible immigration policy that is tied more directly to the work force and would benefit the economy.

Page 48, DAVID PIERPONT GARDNER, with which MATINA S. HORNER has asked to be associated

CED's life-cycle approach represents a significant attempt to come to grips with the challenges of a changing work force and a highly competitive international economy. Only by viewing the problems and opportunities confronting our nation's population at each stage of the life cycle can we hope to produce public policies that adequately address such concerns as training and educating our work force. The CED report provides useful recommendations in these areas, and recognizes the need for the public and private sectors to work together to produce the necessary public policies. I am particularly supportive of CED's recommendations to place greater emphasis on educating students at the primary and secondary levels in foreign languages and cultural studies, to improve access for minority students to our colleges and universities, and to recognize the growing burden that student loans and debt place on our nation's young people.

Page 49, ELMER B. STAATS

Community colleges are playing an increasingly important role in reaching out to the business community to relate training needs and employment opportunities.

Page 104, ELMER B. STAATS

Community colleges have been playing a major role in preparing at-risk youth for the work force, and should be encouraged to continue doing so.

Page 155, ELMER B. STAATS

I suggest an additional point number 10 which would be to promote efforts of community colleges in their outreach at the local level designed to relate training and employment opportunities, recognizing that roughly 45 percent of college enrollment today is in community colleges, a percentage which has grown considerably and will continue to grow in the future.

OBJECTIVES OF THE COMMITTEE FOR ECONOMIC DEVELOPMENT

For over forty years, the Committee for Economic Development has been a respected influence on the formation of business and public policy. CED is devoted to these two objectives:

To develop, through objective research and informed discussion, findings and recommendations for private and public policy that will contribute to preserving and strengthening our free society, achieving steady economic growth at high employment and reasonably stable prices, increasing productivity and living standards, providing greater and more equal opportunity for every citizen, and improving the quality of life for all.

To bring about increasing understanding by present and future leaders in business, government, and education, and among concerned citizens, of the importance of these objectives and the ways in which they can be achieved.

CED's work is supported by private voluntary contributions from business and industry, foundations, and individuals. It is independent, non-profit, nonpartisan, and nonpolitical.

Through this business-academic partnership, CED endeavors to develop policy statements and other research materials that commend themselves as guides to public and business policy; that can be used as texts in college economics and political science courses and in management training courses; that will be considered and discussed by newspaper and magazine editors, columnists, and commentators; and that are distributed abroad to promote better understanding of the American economic system.

CED believes that by enabling business leaders to demonstrate constructively their concern for the general welfare, it is helping business to earn and maintain the national and community respect essential to the successful functioning of the free enterprise capitalist system.

CED BOARD OF TRUSTEES

CED HONORARY TRUSTEES

STATEMENTS ON NATIONAL POLICY ISSUED BY THE COMMITTEE FOR ECONOMIC DEVELOPMENT

SELECTED PUBLICATIONS:

Breaking New Ground in U.S. Trade Policy *(1990)*

Battling America's Budget Deficits *(1989)*

*Strengthening U.S.-Japan Economic Relations *(1989)*

Who Should Be Liable? A Guide to Policy for Dealing with Risk *(1989)*

Investing in America's Future: Challenges and Opportunities for Public Sector Economic Policies *(1988)*

Children in Need: Investment Strategies for the Educationally Disadvantaged *(1987)*

Finance and Third World Economic Growth *(1987)*

Toll of the Twin Deficits *(1987)*

Reforming Health Care: A Market Prescription *(1987)*

Work and Change: Labor Market Adjustment Policies in a Competitive World *(1987)*

Leadership for Dynamic State Economies *(1986)*

Investing in our Children: Business and the Public Schools *(1985)*

Fighting Federal Deficits: The Time for Hard Choices *(1985)*

Strategy for U.S. Industrial Competitiveness *(1984)*

Strengthening the Federal Budget Process: A Requirement for Effective Fiscal Control *(1983)*

Productivity Policy: Key to the Nation's Economic Future *(1983)*

Energy Prices and Public Policy *(1982)*

Public-Private Partnership: An Opportunity for Urban Communities *(1982)*

Reforming Retirement Policies *(1981)*

Transnational Corporations and Developing Countries: New Policies for a Changing World Economy *(1981)*

Fighting Inflation and Rebuilding a Sound Economy *(1980)*

Stimulating Technological Progress *(1980)*

Helping Insure Our Energy Future: A Program for Developing Synthetic Fuel Plants Now *(1979)*

Redefining Government's Role in the Market System *(1979)*

Improving Management of the Public Work Force: The Challenge to State and Local Government *(1978)*

Jobs for the Hard-to-Employ: New Directions for a Public-Private Partnership *(1978)*